LETTERS

Written by

SIR SAMUEL HOOD

(VISCOUNT HOOD)

in 1781-2-3

Illustrated by extracts from logs and public records

Elibron Classics
www.elibron.com

Elibron Classics series.

ISBN 1-4021-3952-7 (paperback)
ISBN 1-4212-9257-2 (hardcover)

This Elibron Classics Replica Edition is an unabridged facsimile of the edition published in 1895 by the Navy Records Society, London.

PUBLICATIONS

OF THE

NAVY RECORDS SOCIETY

VOL. III.

LETTERS OF SIR SAMUEL HOOD

LORD HOOD

After Sir Joshua Reynolds' Portrait of 1783

LETTERS

WRITTEN BY

Sir Samuel Hood

(VISCOUNT HOOD)

IN 1781–2–3

ILLUSTRATED BY EXTRACTS FROM LOGS AND PUBLIC RECORDS

EDITED BY

DAVID HANNAY

PRINTED FOR THE NAVY RECORDS SOCIETY

MDCCCXCV

THE COUNCIL

OF THE

NAVY RECORDS SOCIETY

1893–4–5

PATRONS

HIS ROYAL HIGHNESS THE DUKE OF SAXE-COBURG AND GOTHA, K.G., K.T. &c.

HIS ROYAL HIGHNESS THE DUKE OF YORK, K.G. &c.

PRESIDENT

EARL SPENCER, K.G.

VICE-PRESIDENTS

LORD GEORGE HAMILTON.

ADMIRAL SIR R. V. HAMILTON, K.C.B.

MARQUIS OF LOTHIAN, K.T.

COUNCILLORS

H.S.H. PRINCE LOUIS OF BATTENBERG, G.C.B.
WALTER BESANT.
HON. T. A. BRASSEY.
REAR-ADMIRAL BRIDGE.
OSCAR BROWNING.
PROFESSOR MONTAGU BURROWS.
REV. H. MONTAGU BUTLER, D.D.
LIEUT.-GEN. SIR A. CLARKE, G.C.M.G.
VICE-ADMIRAL COLOMB.
ADMIRAL SIR EDWARD FANSHAWE, G.C.B.
C. H. FIRTH.
DR. RICHARD GARNETT.
MAJOR-GEN. GEARY, R.A., C.B.
LORD PROVOST OF GLASGOW.
DAVID HANNAY.
SIDNEY LEE.
REAR-ADMIRAL SIR LAMBTON LORAINE, BART.
SIR ALFRED C. LYALL, K.C.B.
CLEMENTS R. MARKHAM, C.B., F.R.S.
CAPT. S. P. OLIVER, late R.A.
COMM. C. N. ROBINSON, R.N.
J. R. THURSFIELD.
CAPT. WHARTON, R.N., F.R.S.
CAPT. S. EARDLEY WILMOT, R.N.

SECRETARY

PROFESSOR J. K. LAUGHTON, King's College, London, W.C.

TREASURER

H. F. R. YORKE, Admiralty, S.W.

INTRODUCTION

THE documents contained in this volume are mainly drawn from two sources. The letters addressed to Jackson are taken from the Add. MSS. of the British Museum, No. 9343. The despatches addressed to Stephens are in the 'Admiral's despatches, Leeward Station No. 9,' at the Record Office. A few other documents have been added for purposes of illustration. These are the letters of Lord Robert Manners, quoted from the Fourteenth Report of the Historical Records Commission, the extracts from the log of the Canada, and from Sir Samuel Hood's Journal, and Admiral Graves's account of his action with the Count de Grasse in the Chesapeake, which is taken from the 'Admiral's despatches, North American Station No. 10.' All these MSS., except the first-named, are in the Record Office.

It would, perhaps, be more accurate to say that all these documents, except the letters to Mr. Jackson, are of the nature of illustrations, since it was for the sake of these confidential outpourings of Hood's to his friend that this volume was compiled All the letters to Jackson are not printed here for the first time.

Those of them which deal with the battle of the 12th of April, 1782, and the operations immediately following, are to be found in the 'United Service Gazette' for the 5th, 12th, and 19th of April, 1834. They were then published as contributions to the great controversy started by Sir Howard Douglas's attempt to secure for his father, Sir Charles, the whole credit of the breaking of the line on that famous occasion. To the best of my knowledge the others have remained in MS. until now. It has been thought advisable to reinforce them by official despatches and extracts from logs which serve to throw light upon, or even only to amplify, what Hood said in confidence, and in the bitterness of his heart, to his friend. Jackson was not only an Admiralty official. He had been an agent for Newcastle in electioneering matters, and in that capacity had had dealings of old with Rodney. Apparently, he had what Lord Bacon calls the virtue of a confessor, which is secrecy. Hood, it will be seen, wrote to him without reserve, and so did Rodney. Jervis also was among his correspondents. In the volume from which the papers published here are taken is a letter from the future Lord St. Vincent, containing the curious confession of faith which has been quoted already, though in somewhat softened language. 'I have often told you that two fleets of equal force can never produce decisive events unless they are equally determined to fight it out, or the commander-in-chief of one of them *bitches* it so as to misconduct his line.' In those words lie the explanation of so many of the 'half-begotten battles' (to use Sir Gilbert Elliot's vigorous description of

Calder's action) which were fought from the end of the seventeenth to towards the end of the eighteenth century.

Hood's letters belong to a class of which the student of naval history has to confess that he has but too little. They are not only vigorously written statements of the causes of success or failure, but they give us what is particularly difficult to get in the case of naval men of the older times—insight into motives and character. Official despatches are necessarily somewhat colourless. A man so vehement and passionate as Hood could not, indeed, help imparting something of his own nature to whatever he wrote. But if he had not been sure of the discretion of his friend, or, what is much the same thing, if he had not known that his indiscretions would be judiciously calculated, we should not have this vivid picture of what was going on inside his Majesty's squadrons in the West Indies, and North America, in 1781 and 1782. Thanks to Mr. Jackson's care in preserving his correspondence, we have here not only the official man saying what could properly be said in an official manner, but the natural man writing a great deal which he would have been very unwilling to see published. It is needless to point out which of these conditions is most favourable to the telling of the truth—at least, as it seemed to the man who wrote.

These letters are not only valuable for the light they throw on great historical transactions. They have a biographical, and even a dramatic, interest. Lord Hood was so considerable a man that his revelations of himself must always have value. Moreover, he was so able a man that his judgment of others must always be worth listening to, even when they are visibly coloured by feeling. Nobody who has read the first of the confidential letters to Jackson in this collection can be in the least doubt as to the nature of the feeling which may be supposed to have coloured the judgment of Sir Samuel Hood. He detested his commander-in-chief. The dislike of the second in command for his superior is no uncommon thing in the history of war by sea or land ; but in this case, and at first sight, it is somewhat surprising. Rodney and Hood were old acquaintances. The younger man had served under the older as midshipman in the Ludlow Castle, and then again as captain of the Vestal in the operations on the coast of France towards the close of the Seven Years' War. Rodney had for a time hoisted his flag in the Vestal. This of itself would not establish a presumption that they were friends. But there is good reason to believe that Hood was especially chosen to act as second in command on the leeward station because he was understood to be on friendly terms with Sir George. At the time of his promotion to flag rank, Hood was Commissioner of Portsmouth Dockyard, and Governor of the Naval Academy. The posts were commonly supposed to be held by an officer who had retired from active service. When, therefore, he was appointed to a command at sea, it was generally understood that there must be some special reason for this departure from the common rule. If we are to place any confidence in the word of Sandwich, there can be no question as to the reasons for the appointment of Sir Samuel Hood. In a postscript to a letter written to Rodney on the 14th of July, 1780, he says:—

'I know not what to do to find a good second in command for you; but you may depend on my having that matter in my very serious consideration, and that I will endeavour to pitch on a person who, I think, will be likely to second you properly, and with proper subordination.' (Mundy, *Life of Rodney*, i. 347.)

The vacancy which gave Sandwich so much trouble was caused by the return home of Sir Hyde Parker (Vinegar Parker) from the West Indies in a state of ill-suppressed fury. He was hardly restrained by fear of the King's displeasure from rushing into a pamphleteering attack on his late commander. Rodney, on his part, accused his subordinates, and Parker among them by implication, of deliberately wrecking the battle with Guichen to leeward of Martinique, on the 17th of April, 1780, out of a desire to injure the administration. The merits of that quarrel are no part of the present subject. It is enough to point out that the post of second in command to Sir George Rodney was likely to be a difficult one to fill satisfactorily. The task of the minister was made the harder by what he described as the 'factious' conduct of officers. It had become a fashion to refuse to accept commands on the ground that Sandwich had behaved, or might be expected to behave, ill to the officers to whom they were offered. How far Sandwich was to blame for this bad spirit is again no part of our subject. It is enough that what he called faction, and what his opponents called the proper spirit of men of honour, was very rife. Party feuds, too, were very fierce. In these circumstances the King's minister looked about him for somebody to take Parker's place, who might be trusted not to quarrel with Rodney. That he selected Sir Samuel Hood may fairly be taken as evidence that there was at the time no known personal dislike between the two. That he was especially chosen there can be no reasonable doubt. Writing on the 25th of September, 1780, Sandwich says :—

'It has been difficult, very difficult, to find out proper flag officers to serve under you. Some are rendered unfit from their factious connexions, others from inferiority or insufficiency, and we have at last been obliged to make a promotion in order to do the thing properly.' (Mundy, *Life of Rodney*, i. 403.)

Hood was in the promotion. We need not believe Sandwich on his bare word ; but he was so profoundly interested in the success of the war in America that it is impossible to doubt that he wished, on this occasion, to forward the service by choosing an officer who would be acceptable to the commander-in-chief. Yet Hood had not been five months in the West Indies before we find him writing of his superior in a tone of acrimonious contempt, which cannot be accounted for merely by differences between them as to the proper method of conducting the war. It is manifest from every part of the letters to Jackson, and from much of the more cautiously worded despatches to the Admiralty, that Hood was by disposition a hard judge of others. When we compare his comment on Rodney's excuse for not pursuing the French after the 12th of April with Nelson's criticism on Hotham's almost identical plea for indolence, the difference of tone is as striking as the similarity in the judgments and the circumstances. That fund of 'loving kindness' which is the most beautiful part of Nelson's character softened the terms of his condemnation of his superior. With Hood there is no qualification. Indeed, it is rarely that he has a good word for anybody, or that his criticism is not pointed by contempt. Graves, Rowley, Pigot, Sir Charles Douglas, all came in for their share. Graves is cunning and incompetent; 'our friend Jos,' that is Joshua Rowley, silly; Pigot a nonentity, and Douglas feeble to imbecility. Whatever element of truth there may have been in these various sneers, we feel that they are to be received with caution as coming from a man in whom the inclination to sneer was strong, and who, by preference, was always on the outlook for occasion to find fault. From his own account it appears that he once rated at Sir Charles Douglas in terms which would almost have justified a challenge, considering that they were not talking on service. Something may be allowed for the fact that he had already suffered much from his liver, and that the West Indies is a liverish station, but ill health only makes a man fall on the side to which he leans.

In the case of Rodney this fund of natural censoriousness is reinforced by something which amounts to hatred. He accuses his superior of refusing to allow him to send letters home, of dishonesty in the matter of the St. Eustatius prize money, and in one case (letter of April 30, 1782) insinuates that Sir George was capable of prying into his letters. He calls him a froward child, and accuses him of behaving in the most childish manner over his prize, the Ville de Paris. When we turn to Rodney's own very able letters in Mundy's two volumes, we wonder if these can have come from the same man.

The supposition that something had happened between the two to embitter their relations is one which naturally presents itself. It is possible that it is so. A little thing will do where the superior has a tolerable fund of aristocratic insolence, as was the case with Rodney, and the inferior is as touchy as Hood manifestly was. But it may well be that there was nothing beyond a natural incompatibility of disposition, exasperated by the relations in which they stood to one another. It is never, according to the cynical saying of the lawyers, necessary to seek for a motive for murder in the case of husband and wife. Hatred is only too commonly the alternative to the proper relation. A first and second in command are on a footing to one another which makes hatred very natural, where the superior in rank has not also superiority of faculty, and the power of attracting affection. Hood knew himself to be as able as Rodney and more energetic. Rodney again was a 'stay-on-board admiral,' and did little 'to make a hard and disagreeable service as palatable to those serving under him as circumstances will admit of,' to quote one of Codrington's many, and rather bad-blooded, slaps at Collingwood. We have Rodney's word for it that he looked down on the bulk of his brother officers. 'Sea officers,' he wrote, 'in general, are too apt to be censorious. It is their misfortune to know little of the world, and to be bred in seaport towns where they keep company with few but themselves. This makes them so violent in party, so partial to those that have sailed with them, and so grossly unjust to others. Do them justice and make them do their duty.' (Mundy, ii. 358.)

We have only to suppose, as we fairly may, that Rodney showed a little of the spirit which shines through these lines to Hood, and the dislike of Sir Samuel for his superior is easily accounted for. Hood, though a gentleman born, was not Rodney's equal in birth or breeding. Be the cause of the hatred what it may, it was there, and it must be taken into account when Hood's letters are used as evidence. It gives vivacity and force to his writing, though the flavour is by no means agreeable. There is something unpleasant in the spectacle of Hood writing all these backbiting letters (I am afraid there is no other word for it) while he was keeping up an appearance of friendship to his chief's face. Whatever may have been Hood's superiority in faculty, and in these wars at least it was great, there is an air of breeding about Rodney, a fine distinction of manner, which his able subordinate entirely lacks.

So much for the worst side of these letters, and for that part of them which diminishes their value as evidence or their attractiveness as reading. I have not sought to palliate it. An editor is bound in honesty to give his man with the wart on his nose, as Cromwell insisted on being painted. But the bad is counterbalanced by great qualities. If Hood was uncharitable, it was because he insisted exclusively on what there was to blame, not because he invented groundless accusations. If he was arrogant, he did not look down on other men merely from the height of his own conceit of himself, but from a very real superiority of faculty. When he differs in opinion from Rodney, the result may be held to show that he was right. When he criticises Graves or Digby, the facts show that there was good ground for his condemnation of these officers. His letters are throughout those of a thinking man, of one who was ever for doing the utmost against the enemy. His interest had no doubt considerable weight with him, but then it coincided with those of the nation. He may have longed for command with a free hand, and a sufficient force, as every officer of spirit needs must, but it was in order to win glory by destroying the King's enemies. There is no trace in these letters of resentment because his prize money was interfered with. He never speaks of the war as a means of providing for his wife and family as Rodney did. He never complains that he is making no money while other men are growing rich, as even Nelson may be sometimes heard to do. It is impossible to conceive of him as losing his head at the sight of the plunder of St. Eustatius, as Rodney did, or resenting the appearance of a senior officer with an increase of strength on his station, because it diminished his percentage of prize-money, as Arbuthnot did. No one who is even moderately familiar with our naval history will deny that this is an immense merit in Hood. The appetite for prize money was almost canine with some of his contemporaries. In a letter to Rowley, which is otherwise of no note, Hood asks for the loan of a frigate, with a promise not to detain her for his own emolument. That sentence is very significant in what it takes for granted. Obviously it was not thought superfluous in an officer to assert that he would not subordinate the public service to his own interest. Even zealous men made a great merit of their disinterestedness. Rodney boasted when he sailed for the North American station in 1780 of his own virtue, since he might if he liked have made a rich cruize of it to leeward. Hood treats the whole subject of prize money with the indifference of a man to whom it never gave a thought. His own ease was no consideration with him. To get at the enemy, to get at him as quickly as possible, to get at him with the utmost attainable force, these were his aims. If he had the spiritual pride which the cavalier told Fairfax was the sin of the Puritan and the devil, at least he was not sordid. He would not have allowed two trumpery prizes to influence his movements in the poor-spirited style of Sir Robert Calder. Hood would have sent them, and his share in them, to the bottom of the sea, where he wished the Ville de Paris had gone when he found that she was detaining Rodney from his proper work of pursuing the enemy.

Before going on to analyse the papers in this volume, it is proper to state the grounds on which they have been chosen. The letters to Jackson are given bodily, as being the first cause why the collection was made. The papers from the Admiral's despatches, 9 and 10, Lord Robert Manners's letters, the extracts from the log of the Canada, and Sir Samuel Hood's Journal, are given only in so far as they illustrate the confidential letters which form the core of the volume. I have thought it better to print them all, text and comment, in order of date, rather than to give the letters by themselves, and the illustrations as an appendix. In this way a continuous story is presented. All selections are no doubt subject to suspicion. The student prefers to be allowed to choose for himself, and resents being compelled to rely on the discretion of an editor, who may have misjudged the value of some document. Yet it was impossible to turn the whole of the Admiral s despatches, Nos. 9 and 10, into this volume. Our object also is not to give a complete collection of papers referring to the conduct of the naval war in America and the West Indies in 1781-83, which would be a great undertaking, but only the letters of Sir Samuel Hood, with what other papers seemed likely to illustrate them. I cannot profess to be sure that I have overlooked nothing of value. My selection is presented with the respectful request that the Society will excuse errors and omissions, but also with the confidence that what is given will be found to be of intrinsic value.

The text has been prepared according to the rules of the Society. I have, on second thoughts, decided to leave the italics, of which Sir Samuel made a somewhat profuse use. It seems to me, on carefully going over his correspondence, that he used this now old-fashioned method of reinforcing his words on a definite system He did not scatter italics at random, but underscored the words on which he would, when speaking, have laid the stress of his voice, and to which he wished to call the particular attention of his correspondent. They are, therefore, part of his style. I have, except where there is an obvious omission, on no occasion altered his actual words, even for the purpose of correcting ill-written sentences. Sir Samuel Hood's thought and faculty went to action, not to expression. He can be abundantly clear when he has to narrate or to order, but so soon as he begins to argue he is apt to become confused in his wording. His arguments all endeavoured to come out together, and his sentences became conglomerated. A word inserted here and there, 'to help the struggling sense,' would be of no use in these cases. It would be necessary to break the whole passage up, and rewrite it, turning one sentence into several, to make the wording grammatically correct. But this would amount to a sophistication of the text. The confusion, too, is always in the expression, not in the thought. Nobody who reads carefully can be in real doubt as to what Sir Samuel

Hood meant, and in all cases what he did mean was excellent sense.

I take this opportunity to thank Professor J. K. Laughton for the very great assistance he has given me, not only in correcting the proofs of this volume, but by pointing out to me the sources from which some of the documents have been chosen. No small part of whatever merit the selection may have is to be attributed to him.

The letter which opens the volume has no direct connection with what follows. It is printed mainly because it belongs to the correspondence with Jackson, which we are to give entire, but it has an intrinsic interest of its own. We see from it how soon the news of the unhappy dissensions between Keppel and Palliser had begun to spread. The reports came with the account of that unsatisfactory battle off Ushant, which was the beginning of much evil in the fleet. From it dates the outbreak of quarrels between a large section of the flag officers and the Admiralty, and among the officers themselves, which did us more harm than all the French and Spanish fleets put together. Hood held himself apart from the whole dispute, and to that he no doubt largely owed his promotion and his command in 1780. We shall find him protesting to Jackson that he is neither Whig nor Tory, but only a naval officer (letter of January 29, 1783). His brother officers were in many cases less purely professional in their ambitions. The long predominance of the Whig oligarchy had filled the higher ranks of the service with partisans, and whatever the sins of Sandwich may have been there can, I think, be no doubt that he was disliked quite as much because he was a political opponent as for any other cause. Between this attitude of mind and 'factiousness' the interval is not great. The care which Hood takes to reiterate professions of devotion to the King shows that it was not then taken for granted that an admiral left his party behind him when he hoisted his flag. Hood, in fact, was avowedly 'a King's servant,' and whatever we may think of the action of that party in Parliamentary politics, it must be allowed that they were in their proper place on the quarter-deck of the King's ships engaged in fighting the King's enemies.

The despatches to Philip Stephens, then Secretary of the Admiralty, which follow, have been chosen because they show Hood engaged on work which in war time formed a large part of an admiral's duty, and will, in the future, most probably have to be discharged again, namely, convoy. These despatches show what a tiresome task it was. The difficulty of collecting the ships, the exacting demands of owners, the pigheadedness of skippers, the mere material toil of first collecting ships in roadsteads and then getting them out in the face of the tides and continually shifting winds, made the work as hard as it was thankless. Yet it had to be done. The trade of the country had to be conducted. The commercial classes, which had long been in political alliance with the Whig connections and had become very powerful, would not have tolerated neglect. No English administration would have dared to subordinate the interests of trade to purely military considerations, as the French Government could afford to do. The extent to which the operations of the navy were hampered by these police duties must never be overlooked in judging the conduct of our old naval wars. In this case, for instance, Hood was taking out much needed reinforcements to Rodney. He and his ships were sorely wanted at the seat of war. Yet he was delayed for weeks while his flock of trading ships was being got together by driblets.

'The trade,' to use the phrase of the time, which Hood took with him to the West Indies consisted of 118 vessels of 31,471 tons, carrying 801 guns, with crews amounting to 2,159 men. The West India trade was at that time relatively of very much greater importance than it is now. According to the figures given by Mr. Colquhoun in his *Treatise on the Commerce and Police of the River Thames*, it appears that in 1792, ten years after Hood sailed, there were 346 vessels of 101,484 tons (including repeated voyages, or counting each voyage a ship) belonging to London engaged in the West India trade, as against fifty-three ships of 41,456 tons trading to the East Indies. It will be seen that these vessels were, judged by a modern standard, very small. The bulk of our oversea trade was, in fact, conducted in vessels of from 200 to 400 tons. In Hood's convoy there was only one vessel of over 500 tons—the Dutton, of 700, carrying twenty-eight guns and eighty-four men. She was a hired ship engaged to transport ordnance stores, and was one of the vessels lost in the hurricane which destroyed Graves' unhappy convoy in 1782. The loss of the Ramillies and the Centaur on this occasion is one of the most tragic stories of the sea. The average size of the vessels was only a fraction over 266 tons. They carried seven guns apiece, and eighteen men on an average. If 'men' is to be understood to include apprentices, it will be seen that the number of grown men employed was not considerable. Trouble did not end when a convoy had at last been got out from 'Spithead and the Motherbank.' It had to be protected, and, what was still more trying, it had to be kept in order. Sir Samuel Hood had to complain of the obstinacy of the merchant skippers, and if Beatson was well informed, as he probably was, a dozen or so of them committed what was a very common offence. 'When the admiral drew near to the West Indies he missed in one night no less than twelve of his convoy. It was given out that they considered themselves as out of danger from the enemy, and had proceeded to the various British islands to which they were destined; but when the island of St. Eustatius was taken, Sir Samuel Hood there found his missing ships, busily employed in landing their cargoes to the agents of the British merchants. The masters, mates, and crews of these ships were immediately pressed and put on board the ships of war.' (Beatson's *Naval and Military Memoirs*, v. 160, note.)

In this case the misconduct of the masters was aggravated by the suspicion that they were really engaged in a contraband trade with the enemy; but at all times this practice of pushing ahead of a convoy as it approached its destination was very common. The object of the masters was to secure the early market; but the end of their haste very commonly was that they ran into the hands of the enemy's privateers. The complaints of naval officers on this head were constant, from the reign of Queen Anne downwards.

Hood's first piece of service after joining Rodney was to take part in the capture of this same island of St. Eustatius. Sir George had just returned from the North American station, whither he had gone on the approach of the hurricane months of 1780. His cruize had been very barren of practical results, partly through the sulky obstinacy of Arbuthnot, then on that station, partly through the utter want of any coherent plan of operations, or of faculty for making one, on the part of those who were then directing the war against the insurgents, but also largely because of his own want of health. He had found himself unable to bear the northern climate, and had been confined to his bed at New York. It would make Sir Samuel Hood's letters more intelligible if we could get some account of his first meetings with his superior. The two can have seen very little of one another, even if they had met at all, for the last twenty years. After they had served together in 1760 Rodney had first commanded in the West Indies, and had then been compelled to take refuge from his creditors in Paris. In this interval much had happened of a kind to change him for the worse. He had been embittered by pecuniary loss; by what he considered, and bluntly called, the base ingratitude of man; by the necessity of leading a life of shifts for years. Above all his health was broken. From his own accounts it appears that the gout had obtained such a hold on him that he was often quite unfit to exercise his command. He was now burning with anxiety to retrieve his fortune. He secluded himself much, and it is clear from his letters that he had formed a habit of contemptuous suspicion of all around him. It is possible that his will, and perhaps even his intellect, had already begun to suffer, from the causes which in his last years reduced him, according to a probable report, almost to imbecility. It was to be only too speedily shown that his character had not improved. The fire, in fact, was no longer burning 'in a dry light.' Hood, conscious of ability, remembering old acquaintance, and, as every word he wrote shows, not naturally a humble-minded man, may well have come with the expectation of being treated with friendship and confidence, and upon discovering that he was to be kept at a distance and 'made to do his duty,' have begun to entertain bitter feelings towards his chief.

The war had reached its height when Rodney sailed to attack St. Eustatius. Our determination to enforce the extreme belligerent claim to take an enemy's goods in neutral ships, had produced that coalition of the Northern Powers of which Catharine of Russia was the main promoter, and Frederick the Great of Prussia, whom we had mortally offended by leaving him in the lurch at the end of the Seven Years' War, was an efficient supporter. The Armed Neutrality League had given us the choice between withdrawing our claim to seize our enemy's goods in neutral ships, at least in those belonging to the associated States, or adding to our already long list of enemies the fleets of the Northern Powers, of which the Danish and the Swedish were manned by excellent seamen. Moreover, war with these Powers would have deprived us of the only market in which we could procure naval stores, when the rebellion of the Plantations shut us out from our American supplies. We were compelled to abate our claims largely. It is a passage in our history too much forgotten by those who lament that we have accepted the doctrine that the flag covers the merchandise. The right of search for, and capture of, an enemy's goods, other than accepted contraband of war, in neutral ships may be useful to a belligerent, but it is very grievous to the neutral, and never has been, or will be, borne by states which are strong enough to show their resentment.

In 1781 our enemies had just been reinforced by Holland. The unfortunate Dutch were between the hammer and the anvil. If they joined us against France, as they were bound to do by treaty, they laid themselves open to the risk of invasion by land, where we were assuredly in no condition to afford them effectual help. If they remained neutral we ruined their carrying trade. In this fix, to the intense indignation of Englishmen at the time, but not perhaps unnaturally, Holland found it more to her interest to sympathise with our enemies. On the 10th of September, 1780, the capture, by the Vestal frigate, of the Mercury, a 'rebel' packet, which was on its way to Europe with Mr. Laurens, the envoy of Congress to

Holland, revealed the whole 'perfidy' of the Dutch. A bag of papers, thrown overboard from the Mercury by somebody who was in too great a hurry to weight it, was picked up by the Vestal, and was found to contain the draft of a species of treaty entered into by the town of Amsterdam and the American insurgents. England insisted on satisfaction. Holland equivocated, and sought refuge in the complexities of its constitution, which made combined action among its states difficult. England then declared war, all the more readily because the Dutch, in addition to being manifestly perfidious, were also weak, and very ill able to defend their trade at sea, or their various desirable colonial possessions in different parts of the globe. The position then, at the beginning of 1781, was this. We had not a friend in the world. Austria was alienated because we had helped her enemy, the King of Prussia, in the Seven Years' War, while he would have been profoundly rejoiced to see us well beaten for deserting him at the end of that struggle. Holland had been driven into the arms of France and Spain, which were leagued against us with the insurgent colonists in order to pay off old scores. The whole coast of Europe from the Elbe to the Maritime Alps was hostile, with the exception of Austrian Flanders, which was unfriendly, and Portugal, which dared give no help even if it had wished to do so. In Southern India we were fighting with very checkered fortunes against the genius and energy of Hyder Ali. At no period in the French revolutionary struggle were we in such apparent peril. Our enemies were not menaced from behind, as the French Republic and Napoleon always were. The French and Spanish fleets were better than they ever were in the later conflict. They rode in overwhelming force at the very mouth of the Channel. Our own fleet was not so good, while the necessity we had to maintain large forces in America was a burden we had not to endure till the very close of the great war, when Napoleon's empire was rushing to ruin. If the coalition against us had been directed by a quarter of the genius of the Emperor, it is hard to believe that we could have avoided ruin. Happily, the bulk of our enemies was greater than their vigour or intelligence. Even so our escape is one of the most wonderful passages in our history. When, then, Sir Samuel Hood speaks, as he repeatedly does, despondingly of the desperate position of England, he is not exaggerating, but, on the contrary, using language which might well be applied by a man of high spirit, and clear head, to a situation of extraordinary peril.

For a time the addition of the Dutch to the number of our enemies was apparently rather welcome, as tending to make 'a rich war.' Sir George Rodney received orders from home to seize St. Eustatius. This barren little island, which lies just north-west of our own possession of St. Christopher, or St. Kitts, had become a great depôt of trade. Parliament had allowed the purchase there of colonial produce, in order to obviate the immense inconvenience caused both to the mother-country and to the sugar islands by the cessation of intercourse with the North American plantations.

Alongside of this, and under cover of it, there had grown up a great trade in contraband of war—St. Eustatius was, in fact, pretty much what Nassau in the Bahamas became during the American Civil War. The fact that their opponents were able to procure naval stores in the island was a great grievance to our officers. It was asserted that the Dutch were partial. The chief accusation against them was that after the first battle with Guichen the Dutch had declined to sell rope to Rodney, on the ground that they had none, but had subsequently supplied the French. The fact probably is that the rope had already been bought by the French, or that it was known they would pay better. However this may be, the island was full of plunder, and was seized with alacrity by the English commanders. The story of the St. Eustatius prize-money made a great noise in Parliament and the Press at the time. It was asserted that Rodney and General Vaughan, who commanded the troops, confiscated vast quantities of English goods which were in the island in the course of legitimate trade, or had been deposited there by the colonists for safety. Rodney, for his part, complained that the Government protected English traders who were treasonably engaged in supplying the enemy. It is certain that he was nearly ruined by lawsuits brought against him at home by men whose goods he had impounded. There can be little doubt that he lost his head, and in the desire, of which he made no secret, of restoring his fortune he went a great deal too far.

Sir Samuel Hood's opinion is very clearly given in his two letters to Jackson of the 21st of May and the 24th of June. He thought that the two commanders-in-chief would 'find it very difficult to convince the world that they have not proved themselves wickedly rapacious.' The service suffered grievously. The capture of St. Eustatius was to have been only a part of a series of operations against the Dutch possessions. Curaçao and Surinam were to have been attacked. General Vaughan had, Hood tells us, shown great anxiety to make the attack on Curaçao. Rodney had promised to detach ships for the purpose. When, however, the whole extent of the plunder lying at St. Eustatius was seen, a change came over the views of both commanders-in-chief. Rodney kept his ships in hand. General Vaughan came to the conclusion that, on the whole, the more prudent course was to remain at St. Eustatius to keep a sharp eye on Sir George Rodney. Nothing was done against Curaçao, and Surinam was left to fall before the attack of a squadron of privateers. In the meantime the subordinates, naval and military, stood round in some anxiety as to how much would remain for them. The whole story has an almost comic resemblance to the dissensions which arose among the buccaneers of Morgan's expedition, when that famous commander made his much debated division of the spoil after the sack of Panama.

Hood, who was to have commanded the expedition to Curaçao, was deeply angered by the disappointment of his hopes. He attempted to obtain the support of General Vaughan, but could only extort a dry answer that there were no men to spare. His reply, as given by himself, is most characteristic. '"This is very surprising, General," said I, "for when you urged me so pressingly to speak to Sir George upon this business you did not know but you might meet with resistance here, and have your force diminished; but now you have got possession, without the loss of a man, you fly from your own proposition, which is what I could not have expected from General Vaughan." He made no reply, but turned away and addressed himself to someone else.' So Sir C. Douglas turned away, and addressed himself to somebody else, when Hood demolished his poor little excuse for the failure to pursue the French on the 12th of April. The Admiral's portrait on the frontispiece of this volume shows a face which could look contemptuous. We know from the 'Life of Sir J. Moore' that during the operations at Toulon and in Corsica the military officers thought his manner at times unpleasantly short. When he was in the right, and also in a good white heat of rage, we can well understand that he could snub with crushing effect.

There is only too much reason to think that this wretched St. Eustatius prize-money, by which in the long run nobody got any good, did us infinite harm in the early months of 1781. It was known that a French fleet was on its way to the West Indies, under the command of the Comte de Grasse, bringing a great convoy with troops and stores. The French Government had begun to give effectual military support to the American insurgents. There was every sign that a formidable combined attack was about to be made on us in America. At such a time the first object of the admiral commanding in the West Indies should have been the fleet of Grasse.

His first duty should have been to prevent that junction of the French forces which would give them exactly what they wanted in order to effect our ruin—namely, the power to concentrate a greatly superior fleet on the coast of North America. Unhappily, Rodney acted as if he thought that his most pressing concern was to protect the booty at St. Eustatius. The French had four ships at Fort Royal. Hood was ordered to blockade them with the bulk of the squadron. Rodney kept some ships with him at St. Eustatius. As the island with common care is nearly impregnable, these vessels were not needed. Hood pleaded in vain to be allowed to cruize to windward of Martinique. He argued that in this position he would have a better opportunity of forcing a battle on the French admiral. As Grasse was hampered by a great convoy of merchant ships it is possible—indeed, it is highly probable—that Hood might have broken this expedition up, much as Kempenfelt scattered the convoy of Guichen at the close of the year in the Bay of Biscay. Rodney would not hear of his proposal. The result was that the Comte de Grasse brought his ships round the south end of Martinique, and by keeping between the shore and the English fleet was able to carry them all into Fort Royal at the end of April. Being joined by the four ships already in that port he obtained a superiority of force, of which, happily for us, he made a half-hearted use. Rodney, indeed, complained that Hood did not exert himself sufficiently to get to windward when he did know of the approach of the French. This, however, is surely a tacit confession that he was himself wrong in not allow-ing his subordinate to place himself where the advantage of the windward position might have been more easily secured than was possible when it had to be struggled for at the last moment, and in the night, in the face of light breezes and a westerly current. Hood makes no concealment of his belief that Sir George's fears that the four ships at Fort Royal might, if they were not watched, attack the English islands was a mere affectation, and that his real motive in keeping the fleet to leeward of Martinique was to cover St. Eustatius.

Sir Samuel is no less contemptuous of his chief's conduct during the naval campaign which followed. It was, in fact, a deplorable business. Until the hurricane months the English squadron was engaged in making hurried starts hither and thither, to protect this and that. Its movements were dictated by the French admiral, who kept our islands in a perpetual fret of anxiety, and always contrived to avoid being forced to fight. St. Lucia beat off his attack, but he took Tobago, and the general superiority was with his flag. The truth seems to be that Rodney's health was such as to disable him from command. He had to undergo an operation for stricture at Bath when he reached England in the autumn. Hood's sneering judgment, that he was nursing his popularity, is only an unfriendly way of stating the truth, that he was in no small fear for his reputation. As he must by this time have heard of the outcry raised over the St. Eustatius business, of the attacks made on him in the Press and Parliament, of the lawsuits preparing, and of the capture of the ships carrying home his booty, of which many fell into the hands of La Motte Piquet, it is easy to believe that he suffered from a combination of bodily and mental anguish which might well have broken down the strength of a younger man.

By July all the promise of the beginning of the year had vanished. A crisis was approaching in which vigour and intelligence of leadership, combined with unity of command, would have been required to avert disaster, and they were all wanting. Our forces were divided, while among the leaders there was vacillation, and a complete want of hearty co-operation. The troops in North America, insufficient in any case for the work they had to do, were separated into two bodies, one at New York, under Clinton, the other in North Carolina and Virginia, under Cornwallis. The communication between the two was kept up by sea. As long as the only French naval force on the coast was the squadron of M. de Barras, the superiority rested with us. But if a powerful reinforcement could reach the French ships before the strength of our own was proportionately increased, Cornwallis and Clinton would be cut off from one another, and either would be subjected to attack by the whole force of the enemy. In the meantime our opponents were increasing in strength. The arrival of a division of French troops under the Marquis de Rochambeau had given the Americans an accession of solid military force. Washington had made real soldiers out of a part of the Continental Army by miracles of patience, and hard work. From the beginning of the year he had been planning an attack on one or other of the divisions into which our army was divided. His first intention was to fall upon Clinton at New York, and various tentative advances were made to test the strength of our position. This design was given up for another. Grasse wrote to announce that he had orders to bring the whole of his fleet from the West Indies to the coast of America so soon as the hurricane months set in. It was for this purpose that he had nursed his fleet through May and June, avoiding a battle in which a large number of his ships might be crippled. In this case, if in no other, the French system of subordinating the chance of immediate victory to some 'ultimate object' was justified by the result. The French and American military leaders decided to concentrate on Cornwallis's army in the south, while an inferior force was to be left to amuse Clinton at New York. Grasse was to make for the Chesapeake, where he was to be joined by the squadron of Barras from Rhode Island. The combined squadrons would reach thirty-six ships of the line—a force sufficient to overpower our fleet in those seas. This great combined movement of naval and military forces was carried out with remarkable precision, the only delay being caused by the unwillingness of Barras to submit to the 'commission provisoire' of his junior, the Comte de Grasse.

On our side Rodney and Hood alone seem to have had even an inkling of what was in preparation. Sir George prepared to reinforce the North American station. Until the last moment he would not decide whether to go himself or to send his second in command. His vacillation exasperated Hood, who relieved his feelings by criticisms of even more than his usual asperity. At last Sir George decided that his health left him no choice but to return to England. He therefore went home with the trade, taking several line-of-battle ships with him. Some of them were unquestionably in great need of the dockyard, but we have here another example of the extent to which the necessity of protecting commerce hampered the purely military duties of our admirals. Grasse had stopped the French convoys at Cape François, as it was then called, Cape Haïtien, as we now say, in order to leave his fleet free to operate to the north with its full strength. No English officer of the time would have dared to do as much. As he was leaving for home Rodney detached Hood with fourteen sail to the coast of North America, ordering him to make for the Capes of Virginia. At sea he despatched a sloop with a message to Graves, informing him of the approaching arrival of the Comte de Grasse, and directing him to meet Hood in the neighbourhood of the Chesapeake for the purpose of intercepting the French admiral. Whatever may have been Rodney's weakness at the moment of action his broken health had not dimmed his intelligence. He certainly grasped the situation better than anybody else.

Hood made the land 'a little to the south of Cape Henry' on the 25th of August. He found no enemy in the Chesapeake or Delaware, and therefore went on to Sandy Hook, where Graves was still lying. Rodney's message had not reached him, partly through accident, partly because of the over-zeal of the officer in command of the sloop, who turned aside to chase a privateer, and was himself attacked by a superior force, and driven on shore. Graves made his failure to receive the message an excuse for not exerting himself more promptly to intercept the Comte de Grasse. This is, in fact, a confession that he could not understand his lesson until it was explained to him in words of one syllable. The general situation ought surely to have shown Graves the necessity of exerting himself.

When reinforced by Hood he put to sea, and made for the Chesapeake. But it was too late. When the English fleet, nineteen sail strong, reached the Capes, Grasse was found at anchor within them, with twenty-eight sail of the line. The French admiral at once put to sea with twenty-four of his vessels, and the 'half-begotten battle' of the 5th of September was fought. The despatch of Rear-Admiral Graves, Rodney's comment upon it, and the two papers of Admiral Hood, will put the reader in possession of the evidence required to understand this unfortunate engagement. Apart from its melancholy consequences, it is interesting because it shows us the last forlorn appearance of Article XIX. of the Fighting Instructions, which directs that 'if the admiral and his fleet have the wind of the enemy, and they have stretched themselves in a line of battle, the van of the admiral's fleet is to steer with the van of the enemy's, and there to engage them.' On this formula was based the whole routine system of engaging to windward, van to van, centre to centre, and rear to rear, of 'taking every man his bird,' which hung like a millstone round the neck of the navy for nearly a century. The letters of Hood and Rodney show how the intelligence of the abler men was beginning to revolt against the wooden old method which still satisfied such officers as Sir Edward Hughes, Arbuthnot, and Graves. At a time when we hear of the necessity for the navy of a system on which to fight, it is perhaps well to be reminded of the harm done by the system we once had. It is not the only possible evil of a set of rules of the kind, that they may be drawn up in a dull time, and represent the opinions of some prevalent clique. They inevitably have a tendency to impoverish the intelligence of those who have to use them. Why should Graves, for instance, trouble himself to think when he had a printed book to do his thinking for him? Men, too, who shrank from the responsibility of innovation, as many men of the utmost personal bravery have been known to do, would naturally be chary of losing the protection which they found in blindly obeying the letter of a set of official instructions, even when at the bottom of their hearts they doubted its value.

For some days after the battle Graves remained aimlessly at sea outside the Chesapeake. Grasse remained at sea, with the definite purpose of covering the entry of Barras, who was bringing down his squadron from Rhode Island. So soon as that officer joined him he returned to his anchorage, where he lay with thirty-six sail. Graves, who had been compelled to sink one of his vessels, and was now reduced to eighteen, then returned to New York, leaving Cornwallis at Yorktown cut off from the sea by the French fleet, and hemmed in by land by a force four times as numerous as his own. The rest of the story is easily dismissed. The meagre resources of the New York dockyard made it impossible to refit the ships quickly, and before the squadron was again ready for sea Cornwallis had been driven to surrender, on the 19th of October. History gives no more convincing example of the value of sea power, and of the penalties of misusing the sea power which you have.

The friends of Admiral Graves, acting, we must presume, with his consent, endeavoured to show that he had been badly supported by Hood. The accusation found no acceptance in the service, where it was well known that Hood would have been most willing to take a more active part in the action, if the persistence of his superior in maintaining the line had not kept his division where it could be practically of no service. This is one of the many instances of the kind of sanctity which appears to have attached to 'the line' in the estimation of so many admirals. The Fighting Orders, reinforced by the sentence on Admiral Mathews, had apparently established the belief that to miss beating the enemy was a misfortune, but to disorder the line for the purpose of beating him was a crime unbecoming an officer and a gentleman. His change of commander had brought no good to Sir Samuel. In his opinion Graves should have gone into the Chesapeake after the battle, for the purpose of seizing the anchorage left by Grasse. His own feats a few months later at the Basseterre of St. Kitts establishes the presumption that it might have been done. That Hood would have done it there can be no doubt—still less that he would have succeeded in cutting off the four ships left behind by Grasse, and establishing communications with Cornwallis. Remembering the extraordinary timidity which the French habitually showed in attacking a fleet at anchor, and the many opportunities which chance and weather could hardly fail to present to an officer of Hood's skill and intrepidity, it may well be believed that he would have succeeded in bringing the troops off from Yorktown. More it was hardly possible to do in the presence of such a superior force.

At New York Graves was superseded by Admiral Digby with reinforcements. The change in command was not to any appreciable extent for the better. As the winter months drew on Hood was eager to return to the Leeward Islands. He was no less eager to take with him such a force as would enable him to meet the Comte de Grasse on equal terms. It was in vain, however, that he pointed out to Digby that his ships could be of no use on the North American Station during the winter, when they could not keep the sea; that the Comte de Grasse was returning to the West Indies with his own squadron; that an attack on Jamaica was notoriously in preparation; and that at such a time every available ship should be sent where it was wanted. Digby would not take 'the great line.' Perhaps he could not grasp the situation as a whole. Perhaps even he subordinated the interests of his country to those of his dignity, and did not choose to spend his winter in the position of an admiral without a fleet. Four ships were all that the persistence of Hood extorted from him. Even that reinforcement was diminished in value by the indiscretion of Digby, who allowed the secret of the destination of the ships to leak out, thus depriving Hood of his only chance—a poor one at the best—of surprising Grasse into a meeting on equal terms. Leaving behind him one last letter of bitter reproach, in which anger rendered him all but incoherent, Sir Samuel sailed back to the Leeward Islands with his insufficient eighteen sail. It may be that his tone of fierce insistence was calculated to arouse the obstinacy of those he endeavoured to persuade. Graves and Digby can, indeed, have had no delusion as to the estimate their junior had formed of their intelligence.

The remainder of the papers in this volume deal with the operations at the Basseterre of St. Kitts, the failure to take advantage of the victory on the 12th of April, and the aimless movements of the fleet under the command of Pigot, who by a piece of outrageous jobbery was selected by the Whigs to supersede Rodney. The first and second are among the best known passages in the history of the English navy. The operations at St. Kitts formed the most brilliant episode of the war. Howe's campaign against D'Estaing on the coast of New England, and Barrington's very clever capture of St. Lucia, may to some extent be compared with it, but neither was on the same scale, or had quite the same measure of distinction. Among the officers of the time there was universal agreement with Lord Robert Manners's estimate of Sir Samuel Hood's 'masterly manœuvre.' On such a subject I must, of course, 'speak as a fool.' Yet I cannot help thinking that the whole of the operations around St. Kitts, French and English, are particularly worth studying in connection with the controversy, how far the presence of a naval force on any coast can prevent operations against that coast by another naval force.

It is a somewhat melancholy change when we pass from the affair of St. Kitts to the letters dealing with the feeble sequel to the battle of the 12th of April. For one short interval Hood had been in command, with insufficient forces, it is true, but at least unhampered. In those few weeks he had proved himself the most daring and skilful manœuvrer of his day. The return of Sir George Rodney, somewhat improved in health, but still nearly crippled by gout, brought back Hood to his old insufferable position of having to stand by and see another make a botch where he believed, and had a right to believe, that he could himself have made a masterpiece. All the bitterness of his heart is poured out in the letters of these days. It may seem excessive to speak of the famous battle of the 12th of April as 'a botch.' No doubt it was a famous victory. Sir George Rodney earned his peerage fairly, if only because he commanded on the occasion of a victory which freed England from a nightmare. Still, when all the circumstances are taken together, it is impossible not to see that it was largely gained by accident, and that very indifferent use was made of it. The great controversy which went on about sixty years ago over the 'breaking of the line' seems a little futile when all the evidence is considered. There was no breaking of the line in the sense of a deliberate smashing of an enemy's formation, such as was executed by Howe on the 1st of June, by Duncan at Camperdown, and by Nelson at Trafalgar. The French fleet fell to pieces, and we took some advantage of its confusion. It is to be noted that Hood in his letter does not speak as if, in his opinion, any novel manœuvre had been performed. He devotes himself wholly, after a very brief account of the action, to criticising Sir George Rodney's failure to pursue. Even at the time there was little disagreement as to the substantial justice of the criticism. As for the tone, that has been sufficiently, I trust, dealt with at the beginning of this Introduction. There seems to have been no excess of silliness of which Hood did not think his commander capable, and he has no pity either for his age or his infirmities.

The final letters are a wholesome corrective to the common belief that the victory of the 12th of April was of the nature of a final triumph. They show to how great an extent we were still in fear for Jamaica, and how formidable the naval forces in America still appeared to the best judges. Under the sleepy management of Admiral Pigot the fleet dawdled over even the little that it had to do, but in fact the exhaustion of all parties was bringing the war to an end, and even a more vigorous man might have been unable to do better.

The later operations with which these letters are concerned are of somewhat less general interest than the earlier. When the surrender of Yorktown settled the struggle on the continent of North America, the French applied themselves to what may be described as a merely local campaign. Having helped the Americans to their independence, they now proposed to help the Spaniards to reconquer Jamaica. In return they were to receive the Spanish half of the island of San Domingo. The attack on St. Kitts was a subsidiary operation, undertaken, as it were, to fill up time while waiting for reinforcements, and largely at the instigation of the Marquis de Bouillé. The Comte de Grasse was somewhat half-hearted in his support of the enterprise. The defeat of the combined expedition against Jamaica in the battle of the 12th of April is a fine example of the unwisdom of subordinating the destruction of an enemy's fighting force to an 'ulterior object,' which that very force exists to prevent. In this case, indeed, the doctrine of the 'fleet in being' is well supported by the facts. So, however, is the criticism that the fleet in being must be strong enough for its work, and that the admiral in command of it must not trust merely to his presence to deter the enemy, but must strike at once, and hard. If Rodney had been a timid tactician of the French school, he would probably have thought nervously of what must happen to Jamaica if his fleet was defeated. He would have avoided a battle, would have gone to leeward for the purpose of joining Parker at Jamaica, and would in all probability have allowed Grasse to join the Spanish squadron. Jamaica might still have been saved, but it would have been at a later date, and probably at a greater cost. Herbert's theory, that an enemy cannot act without great hazard while there is a fleet in being to threaten him, surely requires to be completed. It becomes convincing when we add that the fleet in being is so handled as to put him to the hazard—which will hardly be the case if it gives manifest proof of an unwillingness to fight by running away 'to the Gun-fleet.'

After the 12th of April the war in fact died down in America. There were fleets at sea, and they moved to and fro from the West Indies to the North American station and back again, but the combatants were exhausted. The real interest of the war was henceforth to be sought around Gibraltar, or on the other side of the world, where the Bailli de Suffren was proving on the coast of Malabar that it is possible to conduct a long and hard-fought campaign at sea more than a thousand miles from a base. No competent authority will, I presume, assert that the open roadstead of Pondicherry was a 'naval base,' and Suffren had nothing else nearer than the Mauritius.

The naval side of the War of American Independence has not been studied among us as fully as its intrinsic interest deserves. The great Revolutionary and Napoleonic struggle lies between us and it. Being incomparably more striking to the imagination, as well as immeasurably richer in glory; being, too, far more easily known, and full of familiar names all grouped round the heroic figure of Nelson, it hides the earlier war. Yet it may be maintained that of the two the war of 1778–1783 is the more profitable for instruction. A repetition of the French Revolution in the full sense—that is to say, another throwing of all Europe into a witch's caldron, and another Napoleon—is not more likely to recur than the religious wars of the sixteenth century, or the crusades of the twelfth. We cannot hope to see our next enemy disorganised and cowed from the beginning, as was the case with the French fleet in the war which began in 1793. But a repetition of the war of 1778–1783 is comparatively probable. A coalition of Powers whose forces are not half ruined by a great internal social convulsion before the fighting begins is what we have to fear. The American War is perhaps mainly fertile in that kind of instruction which Sir William Napier said was to be derived from a study of the operations of the Spanish generals in the Peninsula—examples of what *not* to do. The French never understood that the best way of defeating us abroad was to crush us at home. We again never seem to have had a glimpse of the truth that the best of all ways of preventing the French fleet from appearing in the West Indies was to keep it shut up in Brest. We did the second best thing—we scattered our forces, we attempted to protect everything, and came dangerously near protecting nothing. It would be rash to conclude that our next enemy will repeat the old mistakes, while it is only too certain that all the influences which induced the Government of Lord North to scatter its naval forces will be at work to make the next ministry which has to deal with a great naval war return to our old errors. The more we can demonstrate the folly of them, the better we shall be able to withstand the clamours of those whose fears for their own local safety blind them to the real interests of the general defence. For this purpose the history of the American War is of especial value.

The portrait of Lord Hood which serves as frontispiece to this volume is taken from the mezzotint by John Jones, after Sir Joshua Reynolds. The original was painted in 1783, immediately after Hood's return from the West Indies, and therefore shows him as he was when these letters were written. I have to end by thanking Captain Charles N. Robinson for his kindness in looking through my proofs and for various suggestions.

LETTERS

OF

LORD HOOD

HOOD TO JACKSON.[1]

Portsmouth Dockyard, 4th of August, 1778.

DEAR SIR:—The Gazette you sent in the express yesterday was [a] great relief to my mind, for an account having reached this place Saturday afternoon of a general action, and my not receiving a line from any one on Sunday night or by the western mail the next morning, though several letters had been received from inferior officers, I suffered very much from my apprehensions that some of those I love may have fallen, but I find no officer was killed. I am sorry, very sorry, the French did not feel themselves bolder, for could all our ships have been fairly brought to action in a compact line, I have not a doubt but the arms of his Majesty would have gained a complete victory.

[1] The letter refers to the battle off Ushant of the 27th of July, 1778. The 'unpleasant disagreement' Hood speaks of is the famous quarrel between Keppel and Palliser.

Inter nos—The master of a Plymouth Trader, that came here yesterday, talks very strangely of reports at Plymouth, of an unpleasant disagreement between the Chief and one of the Vice-Admirals. Has any such account been brought to you? I don't like it; pray satisfy me in this point—and tell me also if your wine is safe in your cellar? I advised you of its being sent hence in the manner you desired [at] the beginning of last week.

Adieu. Affectionate wishes and regards ever attend you and yours from all belonging to, dear Sir,

Your most faithful and sincere humble Servant,

SAM. HOOD.

HOOD TO STEPHENS.

Barfleur, at Spithead, 1st of November, 1780.

Sir:—I beg you will be pleased to acquaint the Lords Commissioners of the Admiralty that *six only* of ships, out of the twenty-eight named in the list you transmitted to me, and for which I am to wait, are yet arrived at Spithead, and from all the enquiry I can make I cannot find any order is received here for the embarkation of the troops.

I am, Sir,

Your most obedient, humble Servant,

SAM. HOOD.

HOOD TO STEPHENS.

Barfleur, at Spithead, 2nd of November, 1780.

Sir:—I have received your letter of yesterday's date by express, acquainting me that the Lords Commissioners of the Admiralty have given directions to Admiral Sir Thomas Pye for causing the first battalion of the 1st Regiment, the 13th and 69th Regiment of Infantry, and ninety persons of General Rainsford's Regiment, to be received on board the West India merchant ships which have been engaged to carry out troops to the island of St. Lucia, and which I am directed to take under my convoy. In return to which I beg leave to observe that the Commanding Officer at Portsmouth has no orders to embark them; and that fifteen of the ships appointed to receive them are not yet come round. Seven arrived last night and this morning, and on the other side are the names of the ships which are at Spithead.

I am, Sir,
Your most obedient, humble Servant,
SAM. HOOD.

HOOD TO STEPHENS.

Barfleur, at St. Helens, 11th of November, 1780.

Sir:—I beg you will be pleased to acquaint the Lords Commissioners of the Admiralty that a pretty large convoy is in sight from the Downs, part of which I know are many of the ships appointed to carry troops to St. Lucia, if not the whole of them. I therefore judged it right to give you notice of it by express, and at the same time to inform you that I shall hold it my duty to put to sea, agreeably to their Lordships' orders of the 4th, if the wind should come to the eastward before I receive your answer. The anchors of the squadron under my command were so buried by the late gale of wind that they were purchased with great difficulty; both viol[1] and messenger gave way in several

[1] 'The viol or voyol block. A large single-sheaved block through which the messenger passed when the anchor was weighed by the fore or jeer capstan; its block was usually lashed to the mainmast. . . . It was only used when other means failed, and, after the introduction of Philipps' patent capstan, was disused.'—Smyth's *Sailor's Word Book*, sub voce.

ships, and the Invincible broke her capstan to pieces; but another will be sent off to her to-morrow.

I am, Sir,
Your most obedient, humble Servant,
SAM. HOOD.

HOOD TO STEPHENS.

Barfleur, at St. Helens, 15th of November, 1780.

Sir:—Herewith I transmit you a list of ships and vessels whose masters have taken instructions for proceeding under my convoy, as also a list of the ships this morning sent me by Lieutenant Parry, in which the 69th Regiment and the remainder of the 13th were embarked yesterday, whose masters have not yet been for instructions. I have left the Swallow and Du Guay Trouin sloops, to hasten them to St. Helens, so soon as the baggage is on board.

I am, Sir,
Your most obedient, humble Servant,
SAM. HOOD.[1]

HOOD TO STEPHENS.

Barfleur, at St. Helens, 17th of November, 1780.

Sir:—The wind being at E.S.E. yesterday morning, I made the signal to unmoor; but the tide running to leeward, none of the ships at Spithead and the Motherbank could come to me till the afternoon, before which time the wind came to south, and blew strong, which prevented any ship from moving. It is now almost calm, but from

[1] An analysis of the list of 'ships and vessels' under Sir Samuel Hood's convoy will be found in the Introduction.

appearances I am apprehensive the wind will be again westerly; not a ship has taken instructions since my last return.

I am, Sir,
Your most obedient, humble Servant,
SAM. HOOD.

HOOD TO STEPHENS.

Barfleur, at St. Helens, 19th of November, 1780.

Sir:—By express at 6 P.M. yesterday I received your letter of the 17th, acquainting me that the Lords Commissioners of the Admiralty, having received a letter from Mr. Long, Chairman of the Committee of West India Merchants in London, informing them that as there are many very valuable West India ships now in the Downs waiting for a wind to join the convoy at St. Helens, he has been requested by several of the owners to acquaint their Lordships therewith, and that it would be a very great accommodation to the trade if they will order a convoy to remain at St. Helens twenty-four hours after the wind shall come fair, in order to give time for the merchant ships to get round from the Downs, and signifying their Lordships' directions to me to leave a ship of the line, and a frigate or sloop for the above mentioned purpose, which I shall accordingly do. But I cannot help observing to you, for their Lordships' information, that it will be scarce possible for me to get all the ships away that are at this port *within* twenty-four hours after the wind is fair, as more than half of those intended to take the benefit of my convoy are still at the Motherbank, and the utmost endeavours of Captain Bickerton and Captain Stoney cannot get them from thence; and none of the ships in which the last troops were embarked have yet been for their instructions. The masters say their not proceeding does not proceed from disrespect to my orders, but from their not being able to keep up their water there. I stated this matter very fully to Admiral Pye a few days ago, and expressed my fears that it would not be possible for me to get away the first day of a fair wind, unless the ships were all collected at St. Helens. The Admiral told me it must be submitted to; that the ships with troops could not keep up their water at St. Helens, or even lay there with safety if it blew hard from the southward, and would be forced to cut or slip and run for the Motherbank. But he was pleased to promise to hasten out every ship so soon as I made the signal to move; notwithstanding which I am very certain it will be the second day of a fair wind before I shall be able to get fairly clear of St. Helens, which will give time for the ships from the Downs to join.

I am, Sir,
Your most obedient, humble Servant,
SAM. HOOD.

HOOD TO STEPHENS.

Barfleur, at St. Helens, 25th of November, 1780.

Sir:—Herewith you will receive an account of the state and condition of the squadron under my command, for the information of the Lords Commissioners of the Admiralty, together with a list of ships and vessels whose masters have taken orders; and I must beg you will acquaint their Lordships that although I made the signal to unmoor at nine this morning, upon the wind coming to north none of the ships, either at Spithead or the Motherbank, have joined me, and several of the masters of ships, with troops on board, have not yet been for their instructions. Such inattention and disobedience is very extraordinary, and the more so as I have left the Guay Trouin to hasten them to me.

I am, Sir,
Your most obedient, humble Servant,
SAM. HOOD.

HOOD TO STEPHENS.

Barfleur, off Dunnose, 2 o'clock P.M., 29th of November, 1780.

Sir:—The wind being at east at ten yesterday morning, I made the signal and unmoored; but there not being enough to stem the tide, the ships at Spithead and the Motherbank could not join me. In the evening a great number of ships were seen coming from the Downs, which were mostly at anchor without us at daylight this morning, when I made the signal to weigh, and hoisted the topsails to quicken the masters of merchant-men on board for their instructions. At ten I got under sail with his Majesty's ships named in the margin,[1] leaving the Swallow, Du Guay Trouin and Fly Cutter to hasten the trade out, and I am now laying to off Dunnose. I am, Sir,

Your most obedient, humble Servant,
SAM. HOOD.

HOOD TO STEPHENS.

Barfleur, at Sea, 11th of December, 1780.
Lat. 46°·14 N., Long. 27°·35 W.

Sir:—I beg you will be pleased to acquaint the Lords Commissioners of the Admiralty that on the 1st instant, at 8 P.M., I received the enclosed intelli-

[1] Barfleur, Gibraltar, Invincible, Princesa, Monarca, Belliqueux, Prince William, Panther, Thetis, and Sybille.

gence from Captain Hope, of the Crescent, from which I thought it probable two of the enemy's squadrons, superior to the one under my command, were cruizing in the ordinary track to the West Indies, and therefore came to the resolution of keeping well to the northward, for the security of the very valuable charge committed to my care. I had also another reason for so doing: that of the chance of falling in with our expected East India fleet, and putting the commanding officer upon his guard.

I mean to keep a northern latitude till I get well to the westward, and to go northward of the island Corvo, when I shall make the best of my way to Sir George Rodney, with five sail of the line, leaving two to follow with the convoy, agreeably to their Lordships' commands. In the act of bringing to, to receive the Crescent's boat, the Belliqueux came across the hawse of the Barfleur; but I am happy to say neither ship is much damaged as to be hindered from prosecuting her voyage.

This accident happened from very mistaken conduct in Captain Fitzherbert, of the Belliqueux. He was in the rear of the convoy, and Captain Hope hailed him before dark, said he had intelligence of utmost importance for my information, and desired he would bring to and receive his boat, which Captain Fitzherbert repeatedly refused, and insisted on Captain Hope's going to me, though he pressed him upon the subject, said he had despatches for the Admiralty of the utmost consequence, and that his going to me would carry him a great way directly to leeward, the wind being at east.

I went on very well and without accident till last night, when it blew as hard at south and south-south-west as I ever knew it. Happily, the gale was of short duration. At daylight the men-of-war and convoy were much scattered, and one ship of the line was seen far to leeward, with only a foremast standing, which I bore down to and found it to be the Monarca. All her ironwork of the main channel gave way, and the mast went by the board. The mizen mast and foretop mast soon followed. She makes no water, but as carrying a ship in her state to the West Indies would be laying her by the walls,[1] I have directed Captain Gell to proceed to Plymouth, and shall endeavour to get this letter on board, though the sea is so high no boat can go to her. The wind is now northerly, so that I have a fair prospect of a short passage. Herewith is an account of the state and condition of his Majesty's ships under my command as received on the 9th.

I am, Sir,

Your most obedient, humble servant,

SAM. HOOD.

ENCLOSURE I.

Intelligence from Captain Hope, Commander of his Majesty's ship Crescent, 1st of December, 1780.

His Majesty's ships Cerberus and Crescent, on the 24th of November, in lat. 42°·45 N., long. 2° west of Cape Finisterre, fell in with a large fleet of the enemy's merchant vessels under a strong convoy; the whole number might be about one hundred sail, among which were twenty-six or twenty-seven men-of-war. The Cerberus and Crescent, being to windward, approached the fleet near enough to discern plainly they were the enemy, but could not with any positive exactness tell the number and force of the men-of-war. They were chased by four frigates, but none of them could come up with his Majesty's

[1] I do not know the meaning of this phrase, but the word is clearly written. Presumably it meant 'by the wall of the dockyard.'

ships. When they lost sight of the fleet they were steering E.N.E. with the wind westerly; the enemy left off chase at half-past two in the afternoon, and stood after their own fleet.

Captain Man and I came to the following resolutions, that the Crescent should go to the northward and look for Admiral Darby, and the Cerberus to the eastward.

On the 26th I got upon the Admiral's rendezvous and found the Bienfaisant, who had parted from the fleet on the 20th, and believed them to be the eastward of him. While in company with the Bienfaisant we fell in with a Dutch ship, from whom Captain Macbride took a mate of an English vessel that had made his escape from Spain, whose intelligence accompanies this. It is evident the fleet seen by him on the 20th is not the same as that seen by the frigates on the 24th, but it is imagined that the combined fleet had fallen in with this convoy, and was bringing them into the bay with some of the ships, for I don't believe the whole force was there. The wind has been fresh easterly ever since the 26th, and I am confident that fleet must still be at sea.

I don't know where Admiral Darby is, but the Cerberus and Bienfaisant are in search of him. Captain Macbride put the mate of the vessel on board the Crescent, and ordered me to convey him, as well as my own intelligence, to the Admiralty without loss of time. Being under Scilly this afternoon, I descried your fleet, and I thought it my duty to give you this information.

C. Hope.

Crescent, 1st of December, 1780.

ENCLOSURE 2.

Intelligence from George Skin, late mate of the Irwine, galley transport, Robert Sampson, master. Captured by the combined fleets in August last, and carried into Cadiz, and on the 8th of November got on board a Dutch ship at St. Lucar, bound to Amsterdam. 'Sayeth, the same day I went on board of a Dutch ship bound to Holland. The collector of the customs at St. Lucar informed the master that he was at Cadiz the 7th, and the fleet, which consisted of forty-four or forty-five sail of the line and many frigates, sailed early that morning on a cruize for seven weeks, which agreed with the information I received from a friend of mine at St. Lucar, but could not learn what latitude their cruizing ground was in. The 9th of November we sailed from St. Lucar for Holland, and on our passage, the 21st of November, about noon, I saw from the deck a large fleet of ships standing to the westward, about seven or eight miles distant from us, we steering E.S.E. in latitude 42°·37 N., and about 20° longitude from Cape Finisterre. I instantly took a glass and went to the masthead to have the best view of them I possibly could. They were in three divisions. The first consisted of fifteen sail, the second of eighteen sail, and the third of twelve sail of the line and eight frigates, four upon each wing. They remained in that situation about half an hour, and then a signal was made from the leading ship of the centre division of blue, white, and red, at her maintop gallant masthead, and was repeated by the whole fleet; then the first and third division brought to, and the centre division bore up and went ahead. The whole fleet then formed a line ahead at a regular distance; the frigates still continued their stations upon each wing, and by their signals and manœuvres I am certain it must be the combined fleets, for that was their daily exercise when I was a prisoner on board.'

1st of December, on board his Majesty's ship Crescent, at sea.

C. Hope.

HOOD TO JACKSON.

Barfleur, at Sea, 21st of May, 1781.

My dear Sir:—By the Ranger cutter, which joined us the 17th, between Antigua and Guadaloupe, I was favoured with your obliging letter of March 20th, and was glad to find I was not totally erased from your memory.

The King has been very gracious and good in giving to his army and navy the spoils of St. Eustatius; and as the Ranger did not sail till the 6th of April, and her commander was in town the day before, I am sorry you did not say precisely his Majesty's pleasure respecting the distribution.

If the Snake brig meets no interruption in her passage to England, which sailed from St. Kitts two days before I joined the commander-in-chief, you will know before this reaches you that I had a *long-shot* action on the 29th of last month, in sight of Fort Royal, with twenty-three sail of the line (to my eighteen), under the command of the Count De Grasse, having Marin[1] and Vaudreuil with him, both *admirals*. The Russell was obliged to quit the line, and seek her safety as she could that evening, but I continued with seventeen sail about three miles to leeward of the enemy, offering to renew the

[1] Marin is probably a slip of the pen for Marigny (Charles René Bernard). Neither he nor Vaudreuil were at this time flag officers. The Count De Grasse himself was only *chef d'escadre* with local rank (*commission provisoire*) as Lieutenant-Général. Cf. Chevalier, *Histoire de la Marine française pendant la guerre de l'indépendance américaine*, 226.

fight, till the next night, when, finding the Centaur and Intrepid could not keep their stations from their leaks, occasioned by a number of shot under water, and that the lower masts of the Montagu, Torbay and Shrewsbury were badly wounded, and knowing the squadron had near 2,000 men [sick and is] short of complement by death, I thought it my duty to bear up, and made the signal at eight o'clock. I never once lost sight of getting to windward, but it was totally impossible; and though the Count had so very manifest a superiority, and his choice of distance, he has, I thank God, nothing to boast [of].

I am perfectly conscious of no one omission in the whole of my conduct, and of having done everything that was in my power for the support of the honour of the British flag. Yet my mind is not altogether at ease, fearing the fate of St. Lucia, though I have the fullest approbation of Rear-Admiral Drake and every captain and officer I have the honour to command, as the enemy landed a large body of troops upon the island, covered by twenty-four or twenty-five sail of the line, many of which were driven from Gros Islet Bay by the batteries on Pigeon Island. The Santa Monica, Sybille and Scourge got into the Carenage, and the Thetis was lost in going in, by the ignorance of her pilot. The officers and men of these ships will be of singular service in the defence of Morne Fortunée, which I hope will be able to hold out till Sir George Rodney can get to its relief.

On the 11th I joined Sir George, with fourteen sail of the line, between St. Kitts and Antigua, having sent four to St. Eustatius to repair their damages. The next day we anchored off St. John's Road for men and stores from Laforey, and to wait the junction of the disabled ships. The 14th at night we sailed, the Centaur and Intrepid being with us, and on the 16th the Russell joined, but we have yet seen nothing of the Torbay; when she comes Sir George Rodney will have twenty of the line, with which I am very sure he will attack the enemy's twenty-four or twenty-five, and I trust a very good account will be given of them. The Count De Grasse is in the Bretagne,[1] and he brought with him three of 80 guns, fourteen of 74, and one of 64, with the Minotaur, Union, and Fier armed *en fleute*; ten of 74 and three of 64 were left in this country last year by Count Guichen. This is the exact force we are to beat, and I doubt not of doing it, can we come to close action. I believe not more than twelve or thirteen are coppered. But is it not surprising that such a squadron, with so large a convoy, should come upon us without our having the least notice, for had a small, fast sailing vessel have left England a fortnight after their departure from Brest, she must have been here before them.

The[2] convoy Captain J. Linzee saw, and very properly sent notice of, was not a part of D'Estaing's fleet, as you suggest, for it was afterwards seen in latitude 25°, on the 22nd of January, and is I fear gone to the East Indies. I tremble at what may happen in that quarter, and am in pain for Commodore Johnstone, but sincerely hope my apprehensions are groundless, and wish him success from the bottom of my heart.

When we weighed anchor from before Antigua, Sir George Rodney meant to have looked at St.

[1] This is a mistake. Grasse was in the Ville de Paris. M. Troude, in his *Batailles navales de la France*, does not mention the Bretagne as present in this action (vol. ii. p. 100). There was a Bourgogne, 74. He does not mention the three vessels armed *en flûte*.

[2] These were the ships of the Bailli de Suffren, which attacked Johnstone at Porto Praya on the 16th of April, 1781.

Lucia, as I understood him, but I now think he is pushing to Barbadoes (where we shall probably be to-morrow) to water the squadron, for not three ships in it have more than eight days, and several not four, which is very distressing to sickly crews. I dreaded what we now experience, early in March, and when I found the squadron and convoy reported by Captain Linzee could not be coming to these islands, I pressed Sir George Rodney to let the ships go into port to refit, and be put in good order, and to give the poor fellows what refreshments we could; for upon turning in my thoughts the length of passage D'Estaing had from Cadiz to Brest, and that he did not reach the latter port till towards the end of December, it was clear to my mind no force of any consequence could possibly arrive from Europe before the middle or latter end of April, when we should have had all our ships in a condition for lasting service, and not one was so. But doubtless there never was a squadron so unmeaningly stationed as the one under my command, and what Sir George Rodney's motive for it could be I cannot conceive, unless it was to cover him at St. Eustatius; and it is equally as difficult to be accounted for by Mr. Drake and every captain. For what solid purpose, my dear Jackson, could the blockade of Martinique answer, for a few weeks only, unless a force was expected to make an attack upon the island? As far as decency and any degree of propriety would permit me with an old friend and acquaintance, I gave my reasons against it, as you will see by an extract from one of my public letters, which I send for your information *only*. I urged him upon the same score in several subsequent letters, and in my *private* ones was still stronger, for we are I believe upon very good terms together; but he was not to be prevailed upon to let me go to windward. Had I fortunately been there, I must have brought the enemy to close action upon more equal terms, or they must have given up their transports, trade, &c. However, I have this consolation, I have no neglect to charge myself with, and on that account I feel quite at ease.

Mr. George Panter, a broker, married a daughter of an old schoolfellow and particular friend of mine, and I am informed is a man of a very fair character. Should you find him to be so, and can be serviceable to him in the sale of some of the Dutch prizes, you will much oblige me. I beg my kindest compliments to Mrs. Jackson, and that you will believe me always,

Most truly and faithfully yours,

SAM. HOOD.

Barbadoes, May 27th.

I will keep my letter open till we get to Barbadoes.

We arrived here the 23rd, and are about to proceed to St. Lucia. The French troops re-embarked with great precipitation on the 13th, between two and four in the morning, and the whole fleet were in Fort Royal on the 16th. The island of St. Lucia was certainly saved by the fortunate arrival of the three frigates, whose captains were very alert. All the batteries were manned by the seamen.

Most sincerely yours,

S. H.

How unkind was it—nay, how illiberal—in Sir George not to suffer a letter from me to be taken to England in the Snake! Strange as it may appear, it is no less true.

Endorsed.—21st of May, 1781. ℞ 2nd of August, 1781.

ENCLOSURE 1.

Extract of a Letter from Sir Samuel Hood, Bart., Rear-Admiral of the Blue, &c. &c., to Sir George Bridges Rodney, Bart., Knight of the Bath, Admiral of the White, &c. &c. &c. Dated 1st of April, 1781.

I begin to be extremely impatient for the honour of seeing and acting immediately under your flag, as I do not feel myself at all pleasant in being to leeward; for should an enemy's fleet attempt to get into Martinique, and the commander of it inclines to avoid battle, nothing but a *skirmish* will probably happen, which in its *consequences* may operate as a defeat to the British squadron, though not a ship is lost and the enemy suffer most. If,[1] therefore, your apprehensions are over with respect to an attempt upon St. Eustatius by a coup de main, and [you] think the Dutch convoy safe from the ships now at Fort Royal, I most humbly beg leave to suggest, with all due submission to your better and more enlightened judgment, whether it would not be more advisable when the whole of the very respectable force you have done me the honour to commit to my charge are watered, stored, victualled, and collected together was stationed to windward, with a proper number of frigates to look out, the chance would not be abundantly more in my favour for effectually crushing any squadron of the enemy's coming to Martinique than by cruizing before Fort Royal. But I most readily

[1] This sentence is, on careful reading, quite intelligible, but the construction is past praying for. To make it grammatical it would have to be broken up and rewritten. The reader will have ample evidence farther on that this great officer was incomparably more at home with a sword than a pen. If I rewrote the sentence it would cease to be Hood's. I therefore leave it as it stands, and shall equally abstain from altering the Admiral's words throughout.

submit to your superior knowledge and experience, and shall cheerfully obey your commands on all occasions with the utmost fidelity.

HOOD TO JACKSON.

Barbadoes, 24th of June, 1781.

My dear Sir:—I have been a long while in anxious expectation of something going to England, by which I should have an opportunity to give my friends an account of my skirmish with the Count De Grasse, for as yet I have not had it in my power to send a single line.

You will by this conveyance have many letters from me, duplicates of which will go in the packet that will probably be home in a week or ten days after you receive this. I have already replied to your very obliging letters, prior to the arrival of the May packet, by which I received three days ago your agreeable and truly acceptable favour of the 2nd of that month. It is quite impossible from the unsteadiness of the commander-in-chief to know what he means three days together; one hour he says his complaints are of such nature that he cannot possibly remain in this country, and is determined to leave the command with me; the next he says he has no thought of going home. The truth is I believe he is guided by his feelings on the moment he is speaking, and that his mind is not at present at all at ease, thinking if he quits the command he will get to England at a time that many mouths perhaps may be opened against him on the top of Tobago, and his not fighting the French fleet off that island after the public declarations he made to every one of his determined resolution to do it; and again, if he stays much longer, his laurels may be subject to wither.

The French have now in Fort Royal Bay twenty-eight two-decked ships, and the Hector at Grenada without a head, foremast or mainyard, which she lost off Tobago, by the Cæsar and her getting on board each other. Sir George has talked two days past of paying a visit to Count De Grasse, and the top-sails are now loose, but I trust it will end in talk only. If it does not, what inconsistency will be manifest? By going to leeward, when if he gives battle to the enemy, he must do it with all their force collected, except one ship, and at the distance the French Admiral pleases, for being to windward in Fort Royal Bay he will doubtless preserve the weather gauge, and if De Grasse should see fit to look towards Barbadoes, Sir George must fight him, let the dis-advantage be ever so great, or the island is gone, and any reinforcements coming be put in danger. Why, therefore, put things to such risk, when no one good can arise by our going to St. Lucia? As that island is now supposed able to defend itself, but even admitting it was not, I am not for having one ship of the line there, and wish the Princesa and Terrible were again with us, for they can be of no use in defence of the island, further than furnishing flesh for manning the batteries, which three or four transports or other small ships, capable of lodging three or four hundred men, would answer the same purpose, was an attack made upon the island. It therefore appears to me most advisable for Sir George to remain here with all his ships till he is reinforced, since by going to St. Lucia he will pro-bably be obliged to fight the enemy under every possible disadvantage; and how will the commander-in-chief be able to reconcile that, after he had it in his power to come to action with the enemy in any manner he pleased, with part of their ships away, unless De Grasse had chosen to seek his safety by flying to St. Vincent or Grenada, which I really believe was what he intended, or else why quit Great Courland Bay,[1] where he could not be attacked with any prospect of success by an inferior force, and had he taken refuge at St. Vincent or Grenada, Tobago must have been retaken?

What a wonderful happy turn would have been given to the King's affairs in this country had Sir George Rodney gone with all his force to Tobago so soon as he might, and in my humble opinion ought to have done! I laboured much to effect it, but all in vain, and fully stated my reasons in writing so soon as the intelligence came. The island in that case would not only have been preserved, but a severe blow given to the French flag, as every ship there with all the troops must have fallen into our hands most easily, two days before De Grasse got there with twenty-one sail. Nay, had he even gone when Mr. Drake did, the island would have been saved, and the enemy could have done nothing with all their force—now they may almost do as they please. But I imagine they will be satisfied with what they have done, and all move to St. Domingo together the latter end of next month, if not sooner, take all the trade from these islands with them, and from thence proceed to Europe in great force, as Guichen did last year. But probably a part of the King's ships may separate off Bermuda and go to Rhode Island.

Our accounts from New York of the skirmish[2] upon the coast of Virginia are told much against the naval commander-in-chief, and by some officers

[1] On the north side of Tobago, between Courland and Black-rock Points. Cf. *West India Pilot*, i. p. 79.

[2] Arbuthnot's action with Destouches off the Capes of Virginia, 16th of March, 1781.

whose character and judgment give weight to them. I am sorry for it. You reckon without your host, my dear Jackson, in imagining an attack upon Curaçoa was prevented by the intelligence sent by Captain J. Linzee. I will give you proof to the contrary, by the following anecdote. Upon my going on board the Sandwich, when we dropped anchor in St. Eustatius Road, General Vaughan took me aside and pressed me very strongly to speak to Sir George Rodney about going to Curaçoa. I replied I did not know how far Sir George's instructions went, but that I would sound him upon the subject; I accordingly did, and was listened to with attention. The next day Sir George asked me if I wished to go to Curaçoa. I answered most readily. 'Well,' says he, 'you shall have five sail of the line and some frigates.' I replied the force was in my opinion full sufficient, and trusted I should make a good report to him. I immediately wrote a note to the General to say I had succeeded with Sir George respecting Curaçoa, desired he would get what information he could of the place, and use his best diligence by means of the people ashore to look out for good pilots, as no time was to be lost. I received no answer from him, and, when I next saw him, repeated the subject of my note, to which he shortly answered he had no men. 'This is very surprising, General,' said I, 'for when you urged me so pressingly to speak to Sir George upon this business, you did not know but you might meet with resistance here, and have your force diminished; but now you have got possession, without the loss of a man, you fly from your own proposition, which is what I could not have expected from General Vaughan.' He made no reply, but turned away and addressed himself to some one else. The truth is, I believe, he could not bear the thoughts of leaving

St. Eustatius, where he fancied there were three millions of riches, as his letter to Lord G. Germain expressed; and I dare say he would have been there to this hour had not the arrival of De Grasse obliged him to decamp. A pretty large sum was levied upon the inhabitants, and some of the captains asked the Commissary-General what the sum really was. He answered he could not say exactly, but something more than 70,000*l.* or 80,000*l.*, he knew not which; and yet there is now, I am told, but 20,000*l.* brought to account. The Lares[1] of St. Eustatius were so bewitching as not to be withstood by flesh and blood (as Lord Clive said in the House of Commons), but tempting as they were, I am abundantly more happy in being at a distance; and it would doubtless have been fortunate for the public had Sir George been with his fleet, as I am confident he would have been to windward instead of to leeward when De Grasse made his approach. With respect to the concerns of St. Eustatius, I am totally ignorant, not having seen any one account, or had a syllable said to me upon the subject. The irregularity and confusion is beyond conception; a quantity of money was brought from the island in the Sandwich, but not a single soul acknowledges to know what the sum is, and a most Flemish account[2] will I am very sure be produced. The Admiral and General have a great deal to answer for, which I told them long ago; and they begin now to be in

[1] This 'Lares' seems to be a piece of pedantry in the taste of the time on Hood's part. The Lares were the domestic gods of the Romans. What Clive is reported to have said is that he was astonished at his own moderation in the matter of loot when in Bengal. Rodney and Vaughan could hardly have said as much.

[2] 'In matters of commerce the fault of the Dutch
Is giving too little and asking too much.'

a squeeze, as many of their actions will [not] well bear the daylight. Had they abided by the first plan settled before I left them, [and] not have interfered, but have left the management to the land and sea folks appointed for that purpose, all would have gone smooth and easy, and to the perfect satisfaction of the two corps; but I now foresee much mischief may arise. The money brought from St. Eustatius was put on shore upon the island so soon as we arrived; and the very day before we sailed (on the 1st instant) with a determined resolution to fight the French fleet, it was all re-embarked, and put on board two of the most crazy ships in the fleet (the Sandwich and Boreas), that almost a single shot in either under water would have sent them down. But the commanders-in-chief could not bear the thought of leaving the money behind them, and notwithstanding they talk aloud of their disregard of money, they will find it very difficult to convince the world that they have not proved themselves wickedly rapacious; and upon what principle do they act in holding out by their conduct that the money is all their own, and no one else has any concern with it? I send you an extract from a letter I lately received from St. Lucia, which I flatter myself will not be unacceptable to you.

The fortunate arrival of the frigates at St. Lucia saved the island, most undoubtedly. Captain Linzee, late of the Thetis, will probably have the pleasure of putting this into your hands, but when he will depart, or in what vessel, I cannot say. He saved nothing but a few shirts, and as he lost his ship in going to the defence of St. Lucia, he has, I think, a right to some consideration, in the same manner as was given to the captains who lost their ships at Rhode Island. If you can assist him in this business I trust you will. Your advice will guide him. Best and most sincere regards attend Mrs. Jackson.

Ever and most faithfully yours,
SAM. HOOD.

Endorsed.—The 24th of June, 1781. ℞ the 2nd of August. Sir SAM. HOOD.

Carenage, 9th of June, 1781.

My dear Sir:—It is with great pleasure I take this opportunity of offering my most sincere congratulations on the very many handsome remarks and expressions I daily hear poured forth from all parties respecting the spirited behaviour and well conducted manœuvres of the British fleet under your command on the 29th of April, which engaged with so superior a force of the enemy's. The first lieutenant of the Santa Monica, who is just returned on his parole from St. Vincents, says that Monsieur Du Plassi, now governor of that island, and who came out with Comte De Grasse, expresses himself in the highest and most pointed terms on the well directed manœuvring of the British fleet on that day, and, to repeat his own words, that Admiral Hood led his fleet like an angel.

HOOD TO STEPHENS.

Barfleur, off Sandy Hook, 30th of August, 1781.

Sir:—I beg you will acquaint the Lords Commissioners of the Admiralty that Sir George Rodney sailed from St. Eustatius on the 1st of this month with the Gibraltar, Triumph, Panther, Boreas, and two bombs, with the trade for England, having the day before given up the command of his Majesty's fleet at the Leeward Islands to me. On that evening I received the intelligence No. 1, and early the next morning Sir George sent me the letter No. 2, and recommended to me to recall the ships he had sent from Basseterre with Rear-Admiral Drake to St. Lucia, and to wait their joining me before I proceeded to this coast.

I instantly despatched the Sybille on that service, with orders for their meeting me at St. John's Road, Antigua, for which place I sailed the next evening with ten ships of the line. In the night I fell in with La Nymphe, which Sir George Rodney had sent to reconnoitre Fort Royal Bay and St. Pierre, and being informed by her commander that he had seen four sail of large ships in Fort Royal Bay, but that the weather was so very hazy he could form no opinion of their force, but thought they were of the line, I instantly sent La Nymphe back with the letter No. 3 to Rear-Admiral Drake. Early the next morning I spoke with an armed brig from New York with despatches from Sir Henry Clinton and Rear-Admiral Graves addressed to Sir G. Rodney, of which No. 4, 5, 6, 7 and 8 are copies.

I sent the armed brig into Nevis Road to complete her water, and then to proceed to St. John's Road. On the 6th she joined me, and, without waiting an hour, pushed away on her return to New York with my answers to the letters she brought.

Having embarked the 40th Regiment on board his Majesty's squadron under my command, at the desire of Brigadier-General Christie, to whom Sir Henry Clinton's messenger delivered the despatches he was charged with for General Vaughan, I put to sea on the 10th at dawn of day, not caring to wait for the St. Lucia ships, lest the enemy should get to America before me; but as I was running out Mr. Drake appeared with four ships of the line, being certain the French had no ships larger than a frigate at Martinique, and without delaying a moment I pushed on as fast as possible.

On the 25th I made the land a little to the southward of Cape Henry, and from thence despatched a frigate with the letter No. 9 to Rear-Admiral Graves, and finding no enemy had appeared either in the Chesapeake or Delaware, I proceeded off Sandy Hook. On the 28th, in the morning, I received the letter No. 10 in answer, and foreseeing great delay and inconvenience might arise from going within the Hook with the squadron under my command.

I got into my boat, and met Mr. Graves and Sir Henry Clinton on Long Island, who were deliberating upon a plan of destroying the ships at Rhode Island. This was an additional argument in support of my opinion against my going within the Hook, as the equinox was so near at hand, and I humbly submitted the necessity which struck me very forcibly, of such of Rear-Admiral Graves's squadron as were ready coming without the Bar immediately, whether to attend Sir Henry Clinton to Rhode Island, or to look for the enemy at sea. My idea was readily acquiesced in, and Mr. Graves said his ships should be out the next day, but for want of wind they are still within the Hook.

Herewith I send you, for their Lordships information, an account of the state and condition of his Majesty's squadron I brought with me from the West Indies. I am, Sir,

Your most obedient, humble Servant,

SAM. HOOD.

Endorsed.—The 30th of August, 1781, Rear-Admiral Sir Samuel Hood.

Received, the 3rd of November.

Answered, the 10th of November.

ENCLOSURE.

Barfleur, off St. Kitts,
2nd of August, 11 P.M., 1781.

Sir :—Captain Ford, of La Nymphe, has this moment joined me, and says there are four sail of the line at Fort Royal. In case you find the report he has made to be true, for he does not seem clear about it, as the weather was very hazy, you will be pleased to remain at St. Lucia, notwithstanding my orders of yesterday by the Sybille, and regulate your conduct conformable to the instructions you received from Admiral Sir George Rodney, as it is impossible for me to give you others at present. I am now on my way to St. John's Road, where I shall wait till I hear from you, and I am to beg you will send back the Sybille and La Nymphe as also the Alcide and Belliqueux, if you think you can part with them ; but I submit that to your judgment, being satisfied you will do what you think is for the best.

I have the honour to be, Sir,
Your most obedient, humble Servant,
SAM. HOOD.

(A Copy.)
Sam. Hood.
Rear-Admiral Drake.

ENCLOSURE.

Barfleur, off Cape Henry,
25th of August, 1781.

Sir :—Herewith you will receive a duplicate of the letter I had the honour to write you by Lieutenant Delanoe, of the Active brig, lest any misfortune might have befallen her in returning to you.

I am now steering for Cape Henry, in order to

examine the Chesapeake. From thence I shall proceed to the Capes of the Delaware, and, not seeing or hearing anything of De Grasse, or any detachment of ships he might have sent upon this coast, shall then make the best of my way off Sandy Hook, where I shall be permitted to anchor or not, as may appear most advisable to you. Annexed is my line of battle, by which you will see the number and force of his Majesty's squadron under my command.

I have the honour to be, Sir,
Your most obedient, humble Servant,
(Signed) SAM. HOOD.

Thomas Graves, Esq.,
Rear-Admiral of the
Red, &c. &c. &c. (Copy.)

HOOD TO JACKSON.

Private. Barfleur, off the Delaware, 16th of September, 1781,
Going to New York.

My dear Jackson:—On the 5th instant, about 10 A.M., one of the look-out frigates made the signal for a fleet, and at eleven we plainly discovered twenty-four sail of French ships of the line and two frigates at anchor about Cape Henry, with their topsail yards hoisted aloft as a signal for getting under sail. Soon after they began to come out in a line of battle ahead, but by no means regular and connected, which afforded the British fleet a most glorious opening for making a close attack to manifest advantage, but it was not embraced; and as the French fleet was close hauled and the English line steered large, the two vans got pretty near, at four, when the signal for battle was hoisted—that part of the enemy's fleet being to windward of their centre, and the centre to windward of their rear. Our centre then upon a wind began to engage at the same time, but at a most *improper* distance (and the London had the signal for close action flying, as well as the signal for the line ahead at *half a cable* was under her topsails, with the main topsail to the mast, though the enemy's ships were pushing on), and our rear being barely within random shot did not fire while the signal for the line was flying. No. 1 contains my sentiments upon the truly unfortunate day, as committed to writing the next morning, and which I mentioned to Mr. Graves when I attended his first summons on board the London. On the 6th it was calm the whole day, and in the evening Mr. Drake and I were sent for, when Mr. Graves communicated to us intelligence he had received from the captains of the Medea and Iris, who had reconnoitered the Chesapeake, which was as follows: That a ship of the line, a 40-gun ship, and a frigate, were at anchor between the Horse Shoe Shoal and York Rivers, and that they saw three large ships coming down the bay, which they thought were of the line. Mr. Graves also made known to us a letter from Sir H. Clinton to General Earl Cornwallis, which he was desired to convey to his Lordship, if possible. The Richmond and Iris were detached upon that service, I fear to be cut off, and think the whole squadron should have gone; they might then not only most effectually have succoured Lord Cornwallis, but have destroyed the enemy's ships there. On the 7th and 8th, the enemy being to windward, had an opportunity of attacking us if they pleased, but showed no sort of inclination for it. On the 9th, the French fleet carried a press of sail, which proved to me beyond a doubt that De Grasse had other views than fighting, and I was distressed that Mr. Graves did not carry all the sail he could also, and endeavour to get off the Chesapeake before him ; it appeared to me to be a measure of the utmost importance to keep the French out, and if they did get in they should first beat us. Instead of that, Mr. Graves put his Majesty's squadron on a contrary course just at dark, and at 8 o'clock made the signal and lay to. At daylight next morning nothing was to be seen of the French fleet from the Barfleur. This alarmed me exceedingly, and I debated with myself some little time whether I should venture to write Mr. Graves a few lines or not, as it is rather an awkward and unpleasant business to *send* advice to a senior officer. However, I at last took courage to do it, and having made the signal for my repeating frigate to come under the Barfleur's stern, sent her with the letter of which No. 2 is a copy. This occasioned another summons to Mr. Drake and me on board the London, when I found, to my very great astonishment, Mr. Graves was as ignorant as myself where the French fleet was, and that no frigates were particularly ordered (for we had several with us) to watch and bring an account of the enemy's motions. The question was put to me, what was most proper to be done? to which I replied that I thought the letter I had taken the liberty to send had fully and clearly explained what my sentiments were, but if it was wished I should say more, it could only be that we should get into the Chesapeake to the succour of Lord Cornwallis and his brave troops if possible, but that I was afraid the opportunity of doing it was passed by, as doubtless De Grasse had most effectually barred the entrance against us, which was what human prudence suggested we *ought* to have done against him. On the 13th, early in the morning, I received the note No. 3 from Mr. Graves, and No. 4

is my answer to it, which again called Mr. Drake and me on board the London. When the resolution contained in the paper No. 5 was taken, there was nothing else left to be done, irksome and much to be lamented as the alternative was. I unbosom myself to you in great confidence that you will not show what I write to a single soul. With every affectionate wish for health and happiness, to you and yours,

I am, my dear Jackson,
Your most faithful and sincere
S. H.

ENCLOSURE I.

Coast of Virginia, 6th of September, 1781.

Yesterday the British fleet had a rich and most plentiful harvest of glory in view, but the means to gather it were omitted in more instances than one.

I may begin with observing that the enemy's van was not very closely attacked as it came out of Lynn Haven Bay, which, I think, might have been done with clear advantage, as they came out by no means in a regular and connected way. When the enemy's van was out it was greatly extended beyond the centre and rear, and might *have* been attacked with the whole force of the British fleet. Had such an attack been made, several of the enemy's ships must have been inevitably demolished in half an hour's action, and there was a full hour and half to have engaged it before any of the rear could have come up.

Thirdly, when the van of the two fleets got into action, and the ships of the British line were hard pressed, one (the Shrewsbury) totally disabled very early from keeping her station by having her fore and main topsail yards shot away, which left her second (the Intrepid) exposed to two ships of superior force, which the noble and spirited behaviour of Captain Molloy[1] obliged to turn their sterns to him, that the signal was not thrown out for the van ships to make more sail to have enabled the centre to push on to the support of the van, instead of engaging at such an improper distance (the London having her main topsail to the mast the whole time she was firing with the signal for the line at half a cable flying), that the second ship astern of the London received but trifling damage, and the third astern of her (the London) received no damage at all, which most clearly proves how much too great the distance was the centre division engaged.

Now, had the centre gone to the support of the van, and the signal for the line been hauled down, or the commander-in-chief had set the example of close action, even with the signal for the line flying, the van of the enemy must have been cut to pieces, and the rear division of the British fleet would have been opposed to those ships the centre division fired at, and at the proper distance for engaging, or the Rear-Admiral who commanded it would have a great deal to answer for. Instead of that, our centre division did the enemy but little damage, and our rear ships being barely within random shot, three only fired a few shot. So soon as the signal for the line was hauled down at twenty-five minutes after five the rear division bore up, above half a mile to leeward of the centre division, but the French ships bearing up also, it did not near them, and at twenty-five minutes after six the signal of the line ahead at half a cable being again hoisted, and the signal for

[1] This is the Captain Molloy who afterwards, in a less 'happy hour of command,' incurred so much discredit on the 1st of June, 1794.

battle hauled down, Rear-Admiral Sir S. Hood called to the Monarch (his leader) to keep her wind, as he dared not separate his division just at dark, the London not bearing up at all.

N.B.—This forenoon Captain Everett came on board the Barfleur with a message from Rear-Admiral Graves to Rear-Admiral Sir S. Hood, desiring his opinion whether the action should be renewed. Sir Samuel's answer was: 'I dare say Mr. Graves will do what is right; I can *send* no opinion, but whenever he, Mr. Graves, wishes to see me, I will wait upon him with great pleasure.'

ENCLOSURE 2.

Barfleur, at Sea, 10th of September, 1781.

Sir:—I flatter myself you will forgive the liberty I take in asking whether you have any knowledge where the French fleet is, as we can see nothing of it from the Barfleur.

By the press of sail De Grasse carried yesterday (and he must even have done the same the preceding night, by being where [he] was at daylight), I am inclined to think his aim is the Chesapeake, in order to be strengthened by the ships there, either by adding them to his present force, or by exchanging his disabled ships for them. Admitting that to be his plan, will he not cut off the frigates you have sent to reconnoitre, as well as the ships you expect from New York? And if he should enter the Bay, which is by no means improbable, will he not succeed in giving most effectual succour to the rebels?

I trust you will pardon the offer of my humble sentiments, as they are occasioned by what passed between us, when I had the honour of attending your summons on board the London, on the 8th, in the evening.

I am, Sir,
Your most obedient, humble Servant,
(Signed) SAM. HOOD.

Rear-Admiral Graves, &c., &c., &c.

Endorsed.—A copy of a letter from Rear-Admiral Sir S. Hood to Rear-Admiral Graves, 10th of September, 1781.

Admiral Graves presents his compliments to Sir Samuel Hood, and begs leave to acquaint that the Medea has just made the signal to inform him that the French fleet are at an anchor above the Horse Shoe in the Chesapeake, and desires his opinion what to do with the fleet, and how to dispose of the Princesa.

London, Thursday Morning, 6 o'clock.

Endorsed.—Copy of a note from Rear-Admiral Graves to Rear-Admiral Sir S. Hood, with Sir Samuel's answer, 13th of September, 1781.

ENCLOSURE 4.

Rear Admiral Sir Samuel Hood presents his compliments to Rear-Admiral Graves. Is extremely concerned to find by his note just received that the French fleet is at anchor in the Chesapeake above the Horse Shoe, though it is no more than what he expected, as the press of sail the fleet carried on the 9th and in the night of the 8th made it very clear to him what De Grasse's intentions were. Sir Samuel would be very glad to send an opinion, but he really knows not what to say in the truly lamentable state we have brought ourselves.

Barfleur, Thursday Morning, 13th of September, 7 A.M.

Endorsed.—Copy of a note from Rear-Admiral Sir S. Hood to Rear-Admiral Graves, 13th of September, 1781.

ENCLOSURE 5.

At a Council of War held on board his Majesty's ship London, at Sea, the 13th of September, 1781. Upon a report received from Captain Duncan, of his Majesty's ship Medea, that they had seen the evening before the French fleet at anchor off the Horse Shoe Shoal in the Chesapeake, that the large ships appeared more numerous, and to be in divisions, but that it was too late to get near enough to form a clear judgment;

Upon this state of the position of the enemy, the present condition of the British fleet, the season of the year so near the equinox, and the impracticability of giving any effectual succour to General Earl Cornwallis in the Chesapeake;

It was resolved that the British squadron, under the command of Thomas Graves, Esq., Rear-Admiral of the Red; Sir Samuel Hood, Bart., and Francis Samuel Drake, Esq., Rear-Admirals of the Blue, should proceed with all possible despatch to New York, and there use every possible means for putting the squadron in the best state for service, provided that Captain Duncan, who is gone again to reconnoitre, should confirm his report of the position of the enemy, and that the fleet should in the meantime facilitate the function of the Medea.

(Signed) THOS. GRAVES.
SAM. HOOD.
FRA. S. DRAKE.

Endorsed.—The opinion of Rear-Admiral Graves, R.A., Sir Samuel Hood, and Rear-Admiral Drake, upon a consultation on board the London, 13th of September, 1781.

HOOD TO JACKSON.

Barfleur, Sandy Hook, 14th of October, 1781.

Duplicate.

My dear Jackson :—I wrote you by the last packet, a duplicate of which you will have by another packet or the Lively. Both have been said to sail day after day for several past. Whichever this goes by you shall have a duplicate by the other, from the desire I have of telling you what really passes here—though, by-the-by, I am monstrous angry with you for not writing me a line by the August packet, as you must know she would find me upon this coast.

On the 24th of last month I attended a consultation of generals and admirals at Sir H. Clinton's, when it was agreed to attempt by the united efforts of army and navy to relieve Lord Cornwallis in the Chesapeake, and I proposed to have three or four fireships immediately prepared, with which the enemy's fleet may possibly be deranged and thrown into some confusion, and thereby give a favourable opening for pushing through it. This was approved, and upwards of 5,000 troops are to be embarked in the King's ships. While this business was under deliberation, word was brought that Rear-Admiral Digby with the Canada and Lion were off the Bar, and as the wind was against their entering the port, I went out to the Prince George next morning early, and had the happiness to find his Royal Highness,[1] and all on board, in most perfect health. I thank God the disabled ships are now ready, and but for an accident of the Alcides driving on board the Shrewsbury and carrying away her bowsprit and foreyard, I imagine all the ships would have been here this day; but I hope and trust they will be down to-morrow, and that we shall be moving the day after if the wind will permit. Every moment, my dear Jackson, is precious; and I flattered myself when we came in that we should ere this have been in the Chesapeake, but the repairs of the squadron have gone on unaccountably tedious, which has filled me with apprehensions that we shall be too late to give relief to Lord Cornwallis. I pray God grant my fears may prove abortive!

It would, in my humble opinion, have been a most fortunate event had Mr. Graves gone off to Jamaica upon Mr. Digby's arrival as commander-in-chief by commission, and I am persuaded you will think so too, when I relate one circumstance only. On the 7th I received a letter from Mr. Graves, desiring I would meet the flag officers and some captains, upon a consultation on board the London at ten o'clock the next morning, and acquaint Captain Cornwallis and Captain Reynolds that their company was desired also. Soon after we were assembled Mr. Graves proposed, and wished to reduce to writing, the following question, 'Whether it was practicable to relieve Lord Cornwallis in the Chesapeake?' This astonished me exceedingly, as it seemed plainly to indicate a design of having difficulties started

[1] Prince William, afterwards King William IV.

against attempting what the generals and admirals had *most unanimously* agreed to, and given under their hands on the 24th of last month, and occasioned my replying immediately that it appeared to me a very unnecessary and improper question, as it had been already maturely discussed and determined upon to be attempted with all the expedition possible; that my opinion had been very strong and pointed (which I was ready to give in writing with my name to it), that an attempt under every risk should be made to force a junction with the troops the commander-in-chief embarks in his Majesty's fleet with the army under General Earl Cornwallis at York; and admitting that junction to be made without much loss, and the provisions landed, I was also of opinion the first favourable opportunity should be embraced of attacking the French fleet, though I own to you I think very meanly of the ability of our present commanding officer. I know he is a *cunning* man, he may be a good theoretical man, but he is certainly a bad practical one, and most clearly proved himself on the 5th of last month to be unequal to the conducting of a great squadron. If it shall please the Almighty to give success to the arms of his Majesty in the business we are going upon, I think we shall stand a *tiptoe*. The Torbay and Prince William arrived on the 13th, a noble acquisition, and makes my heart bound with joy. Why the Chatham is not with us also is matter of astonishment to me. With best affections to Mrs. Jackson,

Ever yours most sincerely,

S. H.

I trust you will bear in mind that I write to you most *confidentially*. *Desperate* cases require *bold* remedies.

HOOD TO JACKSON.

29th of October, 1781.

My dear Sir:—The Ranger cutter joined the fleet yesterday with the August packet from Antigua, by which I had the pleasure of your very kind letter of the 2nd of August, and thank you for it very sincerely. It is a most flattering circumstance to me that my conduct on the 29th of April is so generally approved.

Mr. Graves has just sent me word he is about to send a ship to England. His messenger brings the most melancholy news Great Britain ever received. Lord Cornwallis capitulated to the combined forces of France and America on the 18th—a most heartbreaking business, and the more so, to my mind, as I shall ever think his Lordship ought to have been succoured, or brought off, previous to the return of the French fleet to the Chesapeake, and which Mr. Graves had in his power to effect at his pleasure, after losing the glorious opportunity of defeating its intentions on the 5th of last month; but I have fully expressed myself upon the management of that day in my last letters by the Lively and the packet. I now feel too much, and my mind is too greatly depressed with the sense I have of my country's calamities, to dwell longer upon the painful subject. We are now, I am told, going back to New York to disembark the troops. I do not mean to go within the Bar, and as soon as the troops are out of the ships of my squadron I shall push away to the protection of the West India Islands. I think Admiral Digby would not do amiss if he was to send the greatest part of his squadron with me till the month of March, as he can put them in no place of safety except in Oyster Bay, in the Sound, and they may as well be at Constantinople for any good they may do.

Adieu, my dear Sir. With best affections to Mrs. Jackson,

I am ever and most faithfully yours,

SAM. HOOD.

GRAVES TO STEPHENS.

Admiral Graves's account of the Battle of the Chesapeake.

London, at Sea, 14th of September, 1781.

Sir:—I beg you will be pleased to acquaint the Lords Commissioners of the Admiralty that the moment the wind served to carry the ships over the Bar, which was buoyed for the purpose, the squadron came out, and Sir Samuel Hood getting under sail at the same time, the fleet proceeded together on 31st of August to the southward; my intention being to go to the Chesapeake, as the enemy's views would most probably be upon that part.

The cruizers which I had placed before the Delaware could give me no certain information, and the cruizers off the Chesapeake had not joined; the winds being rather favourable, we approached the Chesapeake the morning of the 5th of September, when the advanced ship made the signal of a fleet. We soon discovered a number of great ships at anchor, which seemed to be extended across the entrance of the Chesapeake from Cape Henry to the Middle Ground; they had a frigate cruizing off the Cape which stood in and joined them, and as we approached, the whole fleet got under sail and stretched out to sea, with the wind at N.N.E. As we drew nearer I formed the line, first ahead and then in such a manner as to bring his Majesty's fleet nearly parallel to the line of approach of the enemy; and when I found that our van was advanced as far as the shoal of the Middle Ground would admit of, I wore the fleet and brought them upon the same tack with the enemy, and nearly parallel to them ; though we were by no means extended with their rear. So soon as I judged that our van would be able to operate, I made the signal to bear away and approach, and soon after, to engage the enemy close: somewhat after four the action began amongst the headmost ships pretty close, and soon became general as far as the second ship from the centre towards the rear. The van of the enemy bore away to enable their centre to support them, or they would have been cut up: the action did not entirely cease until a little after sunset, though at a considerable distance, for the centre of the enemy continued to bear up as it advanced, and at that moment seemed to have little more in view than to shelter their own van as it went away before the wind. His Majesty's fleet consisted of nineteen sail of the line, that of the French formed twenty-four sail in their line. After night I sent the frigates to the van and rear to push forward the line and keep it extended with the enemy, with a full intention to renew the engagement in the morning; but when the frigate Fortunée returned from the van I was informed that several of the ships had suffered so much they were in no condition to renew the action until they had secured their masts. The Shrewsbury, Intrepid, and Montagu unable to keep the line, and the Princesa in momentary apprehension of the maintop mast going over the side; we, however, kept well extended with the enemy all night, and in the morning saw they had not the appearance of near so much damage as we had sustained, though the whole of their van must have experienced a good deal of loss.

We continued all day, the 6th, in sight of each other, repairing our damages. Rear-Admiral Drake shifted his flag into the Alcide until the Princesa had got up another maintop mast. The Shrewsbury, whose captain lost a leg and had the first lieutenant killed, was obliged to reef both top masts, shift her topsail yards, and had sustained very great damage. I ordered Captain Colpoys, of the Orpheus, to take the command of her and put her into a state for action.

The Intrepid had both topsail yards shot down, her top masts in great danger of falling, and her lower masts and yards very much damaged; her captain having behaved with the greatest gallantry to cover the Shrewsbury. The Montagu was in great danger of losing her masts; the Terrible so leaky as to keep all her pumps going, and the Ajax also very leaky, aggravated from old injuries. In the present state of the fleet, and being five sail of the line less in number than the enemy, and they having advanced in the wind very much upon us during the day, I determined to tack after eight, to prevent being drawn too far from the Chesapeake, and to stand to the northward.

Enclosed is the line of battle with the numbers killed and wounded in the different ships, and their principal damages during the action, marked A. The ships in general did their duty well, and the officers and the people exerted themselves exceedingly.

On the 8th it came to blow pretty fresh, and in standing against a head sea the Terrible made the signal of distress. I immediately sent the Fortunée and Orpheus frigates to attend upon her, and received the enclosed state of her complaints, marked B.

At night, about an hour after the fleet had been wore together, the Intrepid made the signal to speak with the Admiral, upon which the fleet was brought too, and I was soon informed that her maintop mast was gone over the side, and they expected the fore-yard would go every moment. These repeated misfortunes in sight of a superior enemy, who kept us all extended and in motion, filled the mind with anxiety, and put us in a situation not to be envied.

I have enclosed the state and condition of the ships, letter C, by which their Lordships will perceive the state of the fleet. To this I must add that the Pegasus joined the fleet from New York, with an account that after separating from Sir George Rodney, in latitude 29° 55′, longitude 59° 33′, having six victuallers and a storeship under convoy for New York, had fallen in with the French fleet and lost every ship, though the captain seems to have used every prudential means for their preservation.

It may not be improper to add that we are without resource at New York, there having been neither stores nor provisions but what has been purchased for many months past, and a very slender quantity even of that.

Several of the squadron from the West Indies being bare of water and provisions, particularly bread, obliged me to supply them from other ships. It being determined in a council of war, held on the 10th, to evacuate the Terrible and destroy her, I took the first calm day to effect it, and at the same time distributed the water and provisions which were wanted. This took up the whole of the 11th, the wreck was set fire to, and I bore up for the Chesapeake about nine at night.

The fleets had continued in sight of each other for five days successively, and at times were very near. We had not speed enough in so mutilated a state to attack them, had it been prudent, and they showed no inclination to renew the action, for they generally maintained the wind of us, and had it often in their power.

The paper marked letter D will show their Lordships Captain Duncan's report of the state of the

Chesapeake, when I sent him to look in the day after the action.

The above-mentioned delay occasioned our losing sight, for the first time, of the French fleet. I therefore sent Captain Duncan to reconnoitre the Chesapeake, who brought me on the morning of the 13th the information which occasioned the council of war, marked letter E, and I sent him again to take a better view, which confirmed the report of the French fleet being all anchored within the Cape, so as to block the passage. I then determined to follow the resolution of a council of war for the fleet, if possible before the equinox at New York, and I immediately despatched the Medea with this packet for their Lordships' information.

I am, Sir,

Your most obedient and most humble Servant,

THOS. GRAVES.

P.S.—Enclosed you will receive a duplicate of my last letter. I beg leave to recommend the necessity for the immediate return of the frigates which may be sent from this country; the want of the Roebuck has been much felt.

T. G.

Endorsed.—No. 7.—Rear-Admiral Graves's letter to P. Stephens, Esq., 14th of September, 1781.

RODNEY TO JACKSON.

Bath, 19th of October, 1781.

This seems the most proper place to print the following letter of Lord Rodney's, written from Bath to Jackson, since it deals mainly with Graves's action in the Chesapeake, which is the subject of the foregoing letters by Lord Hood.

My dear Sir:—This morning I was favoured with yours of the 17th inst., and you may be assured that everything shall be done by me that can contribute towards settling the Eustatius affair, and that when the papers Mr. Crespigny intends reading are presented to me I will execute them as desired, and hope, on my arrival in town, every necessary paper for me to sign will be ready before I leave England, and all money affairs settled to the satisfaction of all parties; but at present I find myself very much out of order with a very violent pain in my stomach, which has continued these four days and reduced me much, which the news from America and Mr. Graves's letter has increased; for it is impossible for me not to feel most sensibly any news which appears to me of the most fatal consequences to my country, and more especially where the navy has been concerned. . . . In vain may plans be concerted to defeat the designs of the public enemy if inferior officers will take upon them to act in direct opposition to the orders and letters of their superiors, and lie idle in port when their duty ought to have obliged them to have been at sea to watch the motions of the public enemy, and prevent the junction of their squadrons. Had Mr. Graves attended to the intelligence I sent him six weeks before I left the West Indies, as likewise to two other expresses I sent him pressing his junction with his whole squadron with Sir Samuel Hood off the Capes of Virginia, he had been on that station long before De Grasse, and, of course, prevented the latter landing his troops in Virginia. The commanding officer, likewise, at Jamaica, had no right to detain the Torbay and Prince William, whose captains had my positive orders not to lose a moment's time (after seeing the Jamaica convoy safe at that island) in joining Sir Samuel Hood at or off the Chesapeake. . . . I likewise pressed Sir Peter Parker to send some of his ships with them, as I was assured the French fleet were intended for that coast, and that, in all probability, the fate of the war depended upon his Majesty's fleet being in full force, and that the blow on which depended the sovereignty of the [oc]ean must be struck off the coast of Virginia. I advised Sir S. Hood by all means to guard the mouth of the Chesapeake, to anchor in Hampton Road if [there was] occasion, to keep his frigates cruizing off the coast to the southward, that he might have timely notice of the enemy's approach, and to despatch one of his frigates to Mr. Graves, acquainting [him] with his arrival, and pressing a speedy junction, no one thing of which has been regarded. The Commander at Jamaica has detained the Torbay and Prince William. Mr. Graves, so far from joining Sir Samuel Hood off the Capes, lay idle at Sandy Hook, and suffered the French squadron from Rhode Island to join De Grasse, which by cruizing from ten to forty leagues from Sandy Hook or by joining Sir S. Hood he might have prevented, and even, when he afterwards joined him, four of his line-of-battle ships were wanting. Ought any man, after the notice he had received, to have separated his squadron of line-of-battle ships? The whole should have been kept in a body, and always ready to act at a moment's warning, and suffered no repairs, but momentary ones, till the campaign was over.

His letter I cannot understand, and his terms, particularly his cut up, a term neither military or seamanlike; it must have been a mistake in printing; he meant cut off the vans from the centre. The other part of the letter contradicts itself, and his mode of fighting I will never follow. He tells me that his line did not extend so far as the enemy's rear. I should have been sorry if it had, and a general battle ensued; it would have given the advantage they could have wished, and brought their whole twenty-four ships of the line against the English nineteen, whereas by watching his opportunity, if the enemy had extended their line to any considerable distance, by contracting his own he might have brought his nineteen against the enemy's fourteen or fifteen, and by a close action totally disabled them before they could have received succour from the remainder, and in all probability have gained thereby a complete victory. Such would have been the battle of the 17th of April had I been obeyed, such would have been the late battle off the Capes, and more especially if all the line-of-battle ships *had* (as they ought) been joined. Our numbers then had been twenty-five, viz. four of Admiral Graves, and my two from Jamaica. In my poor opinion the French have gained the most important victory, and nothing can save America but the instant return of the fleet from New York with 5,000 troops and Digby's squadron; but even then the French fleet will have done their business and gone. If not, block them up to eternity; suffer none to escape from the Chesapeake; they will soon be tired of their station, and wish they had never taken the part of America. I could say much more on this subject, but it is impossible for you to conceive the fatigue the writing this letter has occasioned. I must conclude with saying that if they intend the war should soon be concluded, *there must be* but one General and one Admiral commanding chief in America and West Indies.

Adieu, my dear Sir.

Yours most sincerely,

G. R. RODNEY.

My best respects to Mrs. Jackson.

Endorsed.—The 19th of October, 1781. Sir George Rodney on Graves's action of the Chesapeake.

HOOD TO STEPHENS.

Barfleur, off Sandy Hook, 3rd of November, 1781.

Sir:—I beg you will be pleased to acquaint the Lords Commissioners of the Admiralty that the King's fleet under Rear-Admiral Graves returned here yesterday evening, and as the Rear-Admiral has this day put the ships I brought with me from the West Indies under my orders again, I propose returning to my station for the protection of his Majesty's islands committed to my care, so soon as the troops, army, provisions, ammunition, &c., are disembarked.

Herewith I transmit for their Lordships' information an account of the state and condition of his Majesty's ships under my command,

And have the honour to be, Sir,

Your most obedient, humble Servant,

SAM. HOOD.

Philip Stephens, Esq.

Endorsed.—The 3rd of November, 1781. Sir Samuel Hood, off Sandy Hook. Received the 16th of December. Answered the 3rd of January, 1782. (1 enclosure.)

HOOD TO STEPHENS.

Barfleur, in Carlisle Bay, Barbadoes, 10th of December, 1781.
Answered the 8th of February.

Sir:—I sailed from off Sandy Hook on the 11th of last month, with his Majesty's ships named in the margin,[1] and having previously despatched the

[1] Barfleur, Princesa, Royal Oak, Alfred, America, Invincible, Monarch, Canada, Torbay, Alcide, Intrepid, Montagu, Resolution, Centaur, Prince George, Ajax, Shrewsbury, Pegasus, Sybille, Salamander.

Nymphe and Belliqueux to reconnoitre the Chesapeake, the latter joined me on my given rendezvous on the 16th, and informed me that not a French ship was in the Chesapeake on the 10th. I immediately pushed away for my station, not caring to wait a moment for the Nymphe, and without meeting with any occurrence in my passage deserving notice, I arrived here on the 5th, with all the line-of-battle ships except the Royal Oak and Monarch, which parted company in a gale of wind and thick weather on the 17th. The Intrepid's, Alcide's and Shrewsbury's lower masts ought to be shifted; they were wounded in the action of the Chesapeake, very badly fished at New York for want of proper materials, and were in so crippled a state in the passage that I was compelled to carry a very moderate sail to preserve the masts from tumbling over the side, and there not being a single lower mast for a 74-gun ship in this country, I am securing those of the Shrewsbury and Alcide in the best manner I can, and shall give new ones to the Intrepid.

So soon as the return of his Majesty's ships from the coast of Virginia to New York was determined on, I despatched the Ranger brig with a letter to Commissioner Laforey with the several ships' demands for stores, pressing him in the strongest manner to expedite the Russell and the stores demanded, if he was not certain they could be furnished here, and to guard against any accident that might befall the Ranger. I despatched the Sybille on the same service as I drew near to Antigua; and the Ranger, so soon as she had landed the packet for Commissioner Laforey, was to proceed on to this island with my letters to the Governor and senior captain in the bay, to make known my near approach. Upon my arrival here, and not finding any of the material stores the squadron stood in need of, I sent away the Fortunée that same night to Antigua with a letter to the Commissioner, urging him in the most pressing manner to send the stores as soon as possible; and, by the return of the Sybille to me from Antigua yesterday, I was assured the Russell would be ready to sail as this day, and bring with her the Grand Duke storeship, with all the stores demanded, so that I may reasonably expect them in a few days. But I am very sorry to acquaint their Lordships that the contractor's agent here has not a sufficient quantity of bread to enable the ships of the squadron to go to sea with twenty days each. This is a very serious misfortune, and must prevent my seeking the enemy even if I was superior to them. I have despatched a frigate to St. Kitts and Antigua, to collect as much as possible at those islands.

I endeavoured all I could to prevail upon Admiral Digby to send the whole of his line-of-battle ships with me, as the letters I wrote him, of which I herewith send you copies, will show, but I could only obtain four.

With all his ships, which can be of no use upon the coast of America before the 1st of April, together with a few that may probably be soon here from England, I should have been equal, if not superior, to the Count De Grasse.

The St. Albans and Eurydice, with the Cork convoy, arrived in this bay about ten days before me. I thought it my duty to detain the former, and have sent the trade bound to Antigua, St. Kitts, and Tortola, under the protection of the Pegasus and Eurydice; and, as accounts had been received here that a frigate force was gone against the latter island, I put Captain Stanhope upon his guard against his leaving St. Kitts before he had well informed himself that Tortola was safe.

I herewith send you a copy, for their Lordships' information, of the order I gave to Captain Stanhope.

As a packet was sent away the day before I arrived, with an account of De Grasse's fleet being at Martinique, though it might be reasonably expected I should make my appearance every hour, as the captain of the Ranger brig had delivered the letters I had written to the Governor and senior captain, I thought it right to make known to their Lordships my arrival here as soon as possible. I therefore propose to despatch the Ranger as soon as she comes back from St. Lucia, to which place I sent her to make known my return to this island the moment I anchored.

I have the honour to be, with great truth and regard, Sir,

Your most obedient and most humble Servant,

SAM. HOOD.

P.S.—I was obliged to leave the Prince William at New York, as her rudder required to be unhung, which occasioned me to write the letter you will herewith receive to Rear-Admiral Digby.

P.S.—I have, since writing the above, received a letter from Rear-Admiral Drake, to acquaint me that the bread sent on board the Princesa was so very bad it could not be received, and that the contractor has no other.

S. H.

Endorsed.—10th of December, 1781, Barbadoes, Sir Samuel Hood. Received 7th of January, 1782, at midnight. (4 enclosures.)

ENCLOSURE 1.

Extract of a Letter from Rear-Admiral Sir Samuel Hood to Rear-Admiral Digby, dated Barfleur, off Sandy Hook, 2nd of November, 1781.

When Sir Henry Clinton's and Rear-Admiral Graves's despatches by express to the West Indies, representing the state of things in North America, together with their apprehensions from the united forces of France and America, reached my hands, I did not hesitate a moment in hastening to their relief with every line-of-battle ship under my command, having no more difficulty in deciding then what appeared to my mind most proper to be done than I have now, and I was upon the coast before the enemy's fleet; and, as the present advanced season has removed all further danger from the French fleet from this coast to the West India Islands, it is but reciprocal, and what in my humble opinion the King's service most pressingly and immediately requires, that all the line-of-battle ships you can possibly spare should attend me to the Leeward Islands during the winter months.

With your assistance in aid to the present force under my command, I shall be put in a very respectable state for acting offensively against the enemy, but without it I must be upon the defensive only, and most probably shall not be able to prevent mischief.

I can only, Sir, most humbly suggest and solicit, which is what my duty calls upon me to do, in the most pressing manner; and it must rest with you to decide. As I cannot do as I would, I must be content to do as I can; a man can work only with the tools he has. But I cannot help repeating that not a moment is to be lost in taking your resolutions either way, as I think it necessary I should return to my station at the Leeward Islands so soon as the troops and army provisions are disembarked, unless you have commands for me to the contrary.

I trust you will have the goodness to forgive my entering so largely upon the very serious subject of my letter, as my only motive for having done so arises from my zeal for the King's service.

(Copy) SAM. HOOD.

ENCLOSURE 2.

Barfleur, off Sandy Hook, 10th of November, 1781.

Sir:—I have ordered the three ships you mention in your letter of yesterday to put to sea, and wait for me E.S.E. from the Neversink.

I do not wonder that our intentions, in having it kept a secret that part of your squadron was to accompany me, are defeated; since some one or more have wrote to New York for things, and said they were going to the West Indies. This to me is very extraordinary, as it was so easy a matter to have prevented any captain from knowing it till his ship was at sea. I am most exceeding sorry for it, because it is very[1] immaterial whether De Grasse knows of my going with fourteen or eighteen sail, as he will naturally take care in either case to be four or five superior. Now, had he understood that I sailed with only fourteen, and was found with eighteen by the enemy, great and manifest advantage to the King's service might have arisen therefrom, but it is a great satisfaction to my mind that I have been in no way instrumental in letting the *important* secret forth.

[1] At first sight this word appears to be wrong, but it is so written, and the Admiral probably used it deliberately. He meant to say, 'It is immaterial whether Grasse knows that I have fourteen ships or eighteen, as long as he knows of my real force, since he can be superior in either case.' Digby seems to have thought that he had done enough in giving Hood four ships, and Sir Samuel wanted to make him understand that this was a mistake.

I cannot see it of the least consequence to *you*, which I have often most freely said, whether you know that the French fleet has left the Chesapeake or not before the fleet of his Majesty separates; as nothing can, in my humble opinion, be apprehended from *it* upon this coast for some months to come, and it appears to me of very little consequence whether De Grasse leaves more or less force in this country, since Sir Henry Clinton without hesitation declares he has no fears for New York.

Where can the advantage be in locking up a considerable part of your squadron in Oyster Bay, in the Sound, which is the only place of safety you have for the ships from the weather? And I very much doubt whether they would be *there* safe from the enemy's fire-vessels. Let the army establish what *posts* they may for their protection, and if your ships must cruize in the winter months, where can they be sent *more* for his Majesty's service or your own advantage than to the *southward?* I have already said and written so much upon this subject that I ought to make a thousand apologies for the liberty I now take, and have only to say in excuse that it is solely occasioned by the great anxiety of my mind from the alarming situation of things, not only here but in the West Indies.

I am perfectly sensible you mean everything for the best, and most sincerely hope and trust it will prove so.

I have the honour to be, Sir,

Your most obedient, humble Servant,

(Signed) SAM. HOOD.

(A copy) Sam. Hood.

Rear-Admiral Digby,

Commander-in-Chief, &c., &c., &c.

In Sir Samuel Hood's letter, dated 10th of December, 1781.

ENCLOSURE 3.

By Sir Samuel Hood, Bart., Rear-Admiral of the Blue, &c., &c., &c.

Whereas it is of consequence that the ships bound to the islands Antigua, Montserrat, St. Christopher's, and Tortola may go to the respective places of their destination so soon as may be.

You are hereby required and directed to inform yourself of such ships and vessels as may be bound to either of the said islands, from Captain Inglis, of his Majesty's ship St. Albans, and take them under your convoy, with such others as may be destined to those islands now at Barbadoes, and hold yourself in readiness to sail at the shortest notice. And as I think it necessary to order another ship of war for their protection, you are to take his Majesty's ship Eurydice under your command, whose captain has my directions to follow your orders, and having seen those for Antigua off that island, you will proceed with any bound to Montserrat, and from thence to Basseterre Road, St. Christopher's, where you will carefully inform yourself respecting the island of Tortola, and if you have no reason to suspect that that island is in possession of the enemy, you will without loss of time give your protection to the ships bound thither. But upon receiving intelligence that Tortola has been attacked and taken by the enemy, you will leave the ships bound to those islands at St. Christopher's or convoy them to Antigua, as may be most agreeable to the masters of them, and whether you leave the Tortola ships at St. Christopher's or at the place of their destination, you will return off Antigua, and proceed to this bay to windward of the French islands; and not finding me here, you will make the best of your way without anchoring, after sending your boat ashore to receive the Governor's commands, to Gros Islet Bay, St. Lucia.

Given under my hand on board his Majesty's ship the Barfleur, in Carlisle Bay, Barbadoes, the 7th of December, 1781.

(Signed) SAMUEL HOOD.

To Captain Stanhope, Commander of his Majesty's ship the Pegasus.

By command of the Rear-Admiral.

(Signed) Jos. Hunt.

In Sir Samuel Hood's letter, dated 10th of December, 1781.

(A copy) Sam. Hood.

HOOD TO STEPHENS.

Barfleur, in Carlisle Bay, Barbadoes, 12th of December, 1781.
Answered 8th of February.

Sir:—The Ranger brig came into this bay from St. Lucia yesterday afternoon; a captain of a privateer, a very sensible and intelligent man, was sent in her by Captain Harvey. He was taken by De Grasse's fleet in July last, and had been from that time to the fleet's arrival in Fort Royal Bay, the 24th and 25th of last month, on board the Caton, of 64 guns. He made his escape from Martinique on the 6th inst., and got to St. Lucia. He says De Grasse left the Chesapeake with all his ships except the Romulus, Sandwich, [an] armed ship, and a frigate (of which thirty-four were of the line), on the 4th of November, four of which went to the Cape for the trade De Grasse left there when he departed for North America; that twenty-six sail of the line are in Fort Royal Bay, and four in the Carenage refitting. This information I think it my duty to make known to their Lordships.

It is with infinite concern I acquaint you that the island of St. Eustatius was taken on the 26th of last month, in a most extraordinary manner. I enclose the information that has come to my hands upon the subject, the whole of which has been confirmed to me by an officer who was upon the spot, is now here, and adds many other circumstances. As General Christie thinks it right he should go to England, I have ordered him a passage in the Ranger.

Herewith you will receive an account of the state and condition of his Majesty's squadron under my command.

I have the honour to be, with great truth and regard, Sir,

Your most obedient and most humble Servant,

SAM. HOOD.

P.S.—Since writing the above, the Monarch appears in sight. S. H.

I send you the copy of a letter from Commander Laforey, signifying the arrival of the London off English Harbour.

Philip Stephens, Esq.

Endorsed.—12th of December, 1781, Barbadoes, Sir Samuel Hood. Received 9th of January, 1782, at midnight. Answered 8th of February. (4 enclosures.)

HOOD TO STEPHENS.

Barfleur, Carlisle Bay, Barbadoes, 13th of December, 1781.
Received 9th of January and read.

Sir:—I have the honour to acquaint you that his Majesty's ship Proserpine arrived in this bay yesterday afternoon, when Captain Taylor delivered to me (and went on immediately for Jamaica) their Lordships' *secret* order and your letter of the 1st of last month, informing me that an armament is preparing at Brest of several men-of-war of the line and a large body of troops, supposed to be intended for the attack of Jamaica, when joined by the enemy's land and sea forces in the West India Islands, and that a squadron is preparing by their Lordships of not less than eight ships of the line, to sail with the utmost despatch to the Leeward Islands, to reinforce the squadron under my command, and directing me to consider the protection and defence of the island of Jamaica equally with that of the other islands within my command, and to take every precaution to be well and speedily informed of the motions of the enemy, both at Martinique and St. Domingo, and to make the earliest communications of such information to the Commander of his Majesty's land forces in the Leeward Islands; and in case I should have reason to believe an expedition is meditating by the enemy against Jamaica, to send immediate notice thereof to the Governor of that island, and to the Commander of his Majesty's ships there; and in the mean time to consult with the commander of his Majesty's land forces here, the best means of succouring the said island if it should be attacked; and so soon as I shall be informed of the actual sailing of the enemy for that purpose to take on board his Majesty's ships under my command such a detachment of the land forces as the Commander here shall judge proper to send, and to proceed with the whole of my squadron, or to detach such part of it as, from the intelligence I may have received of the naval force of the enemy, I shall judge necessary and sufficient for the relief of Jamaica—all which, with the other parts of the said secret order and letter, I shall not fail to pay the utmost attention to; and if I can get only a month's bread for the squadron under my command, when it is put in a condition for service, I will certainly sail, and use my best endeavours to intercept the armament from Brest before it reaches Martinique, taking all the care I am able to be informed as expeditiously as possible of any movement of the enemy's fleet under De Grasse; but if no bread can be got at Antigua or St. Kitts, I shall from necessity be compelled to remain in this bay, or go no farther than St. Lucia till a convoy arrives from England. I have ordered the ships' companies of the squadron to half allowance of bread, and flour to be issued in lieu. The Monarch is just anchored.

I have the honour to be, with great truth and esteem, Sir,

Your most obedient and most humble Servant,

SAM. HOOD.

Philip Stephens, Esq.

Endorsed.—13th of December, 1781, Barbadoes, Sir Samuel Hood. Received 9th of January, 1782, at midnight.

HOOD TO STEPHENS.

Barfleur, at Sea, 20th of January, 1782.
Received 12th of March, 1782.

Sir:—Herewith you will receive duplicates of my letters by the Ranger brig.

On the 25th of November Count De Grasse returned to Martinique with thirty sail of the line, the Experiment, and several frigates, since which the Sagittaire and two frigates have joined from Boston, four sail of the line went to the Cape.

On the 5th of last month I arrived at Barbadoes with sixteen sail of the line, the Royal Oak and Monarch having parted company. I found the St. Albans in Carlisle Bay, which I thought my duty to detain, and take under my orders for the present.

The Monarch joined me on the 12th of last month, and La Nymphe on the 24th, by whose Commander I learnt that he left the Royal Oak at St. Kitts, in a most wretched state. She is since got to English Harbour, and is now there without a lower mast.

The contractor's agent for victualling his Majesty's navy was without bread, pease, or flour. I have *borrowed* of the army the two last articles, as far as General Christie could *lend*; but not a pound of bread was to be got, of which the squadron has been at half allowance for several weeks, has now but fourteen days, and only flour in that proportion. I know nothing of the contractor, but have no good opinion of his Barbadoes agent.

The whole of the French fleet appeared off St. Lucia on the 17th of last month, endeavouring to get to windward, and having carried away many top-masts and yards in struggling [against] very squally weather, returned to Fort Royal Bay on the 23rd in the evening, and on the 28th came out again with upwards of forty transports manœuvring as before, but without making an attempt to land. On the 2nd instant it again left St. Lucia, and stood over towards Martinique. Captain Harvey, who commanded at St. Lucia, had my order to watch the enemy's motions *daily*; to send two frigates on that service, one to follow the French fleet, and the other to return to me.

On the 8th the Lizard joined, and I was informed by Captain Dodd, her commander, that the whole of the enemy's fleet except *one* had sailed on the 5th, and that the Triton was following them.

I sent away the Lizard immediately, to go first to Antigua and then to St. Kitts to gain intelligence, and to assure the commanding officers, both civil and military, that I would hasten to their relief the moment I heard an attack was made. Inferior as I was, I had sent the same message to General St. Leger upon the enemy's first appearing off St. Lucia. On the 10th I received information from Captain Harvey that the Triton was returned, having sprung her foremast very badly off Dominica, and without any account of the enemy; and on the 12th a vessel came in from St. Kitts which left it on the 9th, when nothing had been there seen or heard of an enemy's fleet.

Commodore Affleck arrived in the Bedford from New York on the 12th.

The Prudent sailed with him, but parted company.

On the 14th I received a letter from Governor Shirley, by a despatch vessel, dated St. Kitts, the 10th, informing me a very large fleet of men-of-war and transports had that day been seen from the hills of Nevis.

I immediately put to sea, and next morning very luckily joined the Russell, which was at St. Kitts with the Whitby armed ship when the account was received of the enemy's fleet having been seen. Captain Stanhope sailed that night, but has seen nothing of the Whitby since, in which are stores for the squadron very much wanted. The Russell with the storeship left English Harbour the *first* time on the 13th of last month, and put back on the 21st with her main and foremast very badly sprung; afterwards broke from her moorings, tailed on shore, and beat her rudder and false keel off. Her mainmast being shifted and her foremast fished, she sailed a *second* time with the Whitby, and by one accident and another was carried to St. Kitts.

On the 16th the Lizard joined me, with an account that the French fleet had invested St. Kitts, that the Prudent was at English Harbour, and that the Robust and Janus had put in there in the greatest distress, it being with much labour and fatigue they could be kept from sinking.

Nothing but flattering winds from North by East to North-East by Fast since I sailed, with much swell, and an ugly sea at *times*. The Monarch and Russell has each lost a maintopsail yard, and yesterday afternoon, when I bid fair for leading round Deseada, the Shrewsbury carried away her main and mizen topmast and main topsail yard. I have sent two frigates on before to make known our *greatest* wants, and those that *must* be supplied, to Commissioner Laforey, which I dare say will be ready the moment I appear off.

When the President joins I shall be twenty-two strong, with which I beg you will assure their Lordships I will seek and give battle to the Count De Grasse, be his numbers as they may.

I have the honour to be, with great truth and regard, Sir,

Your most obedient and most humble Servant,

SAM. HOOD,

HOOD TO STEPHENS.

Barfleur, in Basseterre Road, St. Christopher's,
6th of February, 1782. Received 12th of March, 1782.

Sir :—I am sorry to acquaint you that his Majesty's ship Solebay was run on shore and lost on Nevis Point, in coming into this road on the 25th of last month, and herewith I transmit a copy of Captain Everett's letter giving an account of his misfortune.

I am also further to acquaint you, for their Lordships' information, that as it appears to me there must have been great neglect somewhere when the Alfred ran on board La Nymphe, I have directed the officer of the watch in each ship to be suspended, and shall order them to be tried at a court-martial so soon as it can be conveniently done.

I have the honour to be, Sir,
Your most obedient and most humble Servant,
SAM. HOOD.

HOOD TO STEPHENS.

Barfleur, Basseterre Road, St. Kitts,
8th of January, 1782. [Should be February.]
Received 12th of March, 1782.

Sir:—In consequence of Captain Stanhope's ill state of health, I yesterday consented to an exchange between Captain Saumarez of the Tisiphone and him, as he could not possibly live in this country. At three in the morning the Tisiphone weighed to get up to windward, in order to push through the channel of the narrows between Nevis and St. Christopher's at the dawn of day, but from Captain Stanhope's not being able to attend to his duty, and through mismanagement, the ship instead of getting to windward went to leeward, and must have been taken had the enemy's fleet been as near as usual at daylight. This put me under the necessity of sending for my despatches, not thinking them safe while the ship had a captain unequal to his duty from want of health. This was a very painful circumstance to me, from the knowledge I had of Captain Stanhope's zeal and assiduity in his Majesty's service, but I thought myself obliged to do it. In consequence of which I received the letter of which the enclosed is a copy from Captain Stanhope, and have appointed Mr. Sandys to be captain of the Tisiphone, which I hope their Lordships will approve; and from a desire of gratifying the wishes of almost a dying officer, I have continued my despatches in Captain Stanhope's care, to deliver if he is able.

I have the honour to be, Sir,
Your most obedient, humble Servant,
SAM. HOOD.

Philip Stephens, Esq.

NOTE.—Captain Stanhope commanded the Russell, 74. An account of the extraordinary stroke of good fortune by which Lord de Saumarez obtained the command of a line-of-battle ship on 'the station for honour,' as Nelson called the West Indies, at the age of twenty-five, and in the midst of the most brilliant passage of the American War, will be found in Sir J. Ross's life of him, i. pp. 61, 63.

FROM THE LOG OF H.M.S CANADA.[1]

Monday, 21*st* [*Jany.* 1782].—Fresh breezes and clear; P.M. at 5 saw a sail off Guadaloupe standing to the southward; at 6 Antigua bore from W. and N. to N.W. and N.; at 12 the Admiral made the signal to tack; made and shortened sail occasionally; A.M. at 1 wore; at 3 the Admiral made the signal to tack; fresh breezes and cloudy with rain; tacked pr. signal; at 6 the northernmost part of Antigua, N.W. and N. 4 or 5 miles; at 7 bore away; at 5 min. pt. 7 brought to; Montserrat S.W. and W. ½ W. 7 or 8 leagues; the Admiral made the signal for all Lieutenants; the Convert made sail to leeward; the Prudent, Sybille,

[1] It may not be out of place to recall the old rule by which logs were dated from mid-day to mid-day. Thus the 21st of January in this case begins at 12 o'clock on the 20th.

and Drake sloop came out of English Harbour and joined the fleet; at 10 the Admiral made the signal for all flag officers; in company with the Admiral and fleet.

Tuesday, 22*nd.*—At anchor in St. John's Road, Antigua.—Fresh breezes and cloudy; P.M. in boats, and made sail; ½ pt. 2 the Admiral made the Intrepid's signal to keep more away, and at 3 the signal to prepare to anchor; ½ pt. 3 the Admiral made the signal to tack; tacked occasionally, working into St. John's Road; at 7 came to anchor in St. John's Road in company wth the Admiral and fleet; Sister Islands bearing N.E. and E. and St. John's Fort S.E. and E. ½ E.; the Five Islands S. and W.; A.M. fresh breezes and clear; hoisted out the long-boat; sent 10 butts of water on board H.M. ship Russell, and received casks in lieu; received sundry sails from H.M. ship Prudent.

Wednesday, 23*rd.*—Fresh breezes and clear; P.M. received on board 50 barrels of flour; A.M. at 6 the Admiral made the Shrewsbury's signal for a lieutenant; at 9 he made the signal for all midshipmen; ¼ pt. 9 he made the signal for all flag officers, and the Alcides and Centaur's signals for their captains and the signal for all lieutenants.

Thursday, 24*th.*—Moderate and clear; P.M. at 4 the Admirals and Commodores made the signals for all captains of their divisions; at 5 came to sail in company with the Admiral and fleet; at sunset the south-west-most part of Nevis W. by So., the north-west-most part of St. Kitts N.N.W., and Rock Redondo W.S.W.; La Nymphe and La Fortunée made sail to leeward; made and shortened sail occasionally; A.M. squally with rain; ½ pt. 1 brought to head to the southward; at 4 the Admiral made the signal to bear up; at 7 observed the Alfred with her fore topmast down, and jib boom and sprit-sailyard gone, and being much damaged about the bows appeared as if some ship had run on board of her; she fired several guns and made the signal to speak the Admiral; at 8 the Admiral made the Alfred's signal to come within hail; at 10 one of our frigates to leeward made the signal to speak the Admiral; ½ pt. 11 the Admiral made the signal for all cruizers; 2 French ships in sight; observed a cutter working into the fleet, with English colours hoisted over French; at noon saw 2 more enemy's ships from the deck and 7 from the masthead; Rock Redondo S.E. and E., and Antigua E. ½ No. In company with the Admiral and fleet.

Friday, 25*th*.—P.M. moderate and clear; at 2 bore up and run to leeward of the Admiral; the Admiral made the Alfred's and St. Albans signals to change stations in the line of battle and La Nymphe's signal for her captain; ½ pt. 5 the Centaur made the signal for a fleet in the N.W.; at 6 Rock Redondo E.N.E. and the north-west-most part of Nevis N.W. ½ W.; at 8 the Admiral made the signal to make sail after lying by; ¾ pt. 9 he made the signal to tack; made and shortened sail occasionally; at 20 min. past 10 tacked; moderate and clear; A.M. ½ pt. saw the enemies fleet to leeward, they fired several guns and threw up rockets; ½ pt. 3 tacked pr. signal; the French fleet made the signal and tacked; at 4 the Admiral made the signal to tack; ½ pt. 5 he made the signal to form the line of battle upon the starboard, tacked two cables' length asunder; at 7 tacked and brought to in our station; at 45 min. pt. 9 the Admiral made the signal to bring to the sternmost ships first; at 5 min. pt. 11 filled per signal the van first; ¼ pt. 11 the Admiral made the signal for the leading ships to make the same sail he did; the Admiral set his topsails, foresail, jib, and staysail; at 25 min. pt. 11 he made the signal that the rear were at too great a distance from the centre; at 40 min. pt. 11 he repeated this signal; at 55 min. pt. 11 he made the signal to prepare to anchor; put springs upon our cables; we made and shortened sail occasionally; at noon, moderate and clear; the Admiral made sundry other signals occasionally. In company with the Admiral and fleet.

Saturday, 26*th*.—Running along the high land of Nevis.—P.M. running along shore in line of battle ahead; at 20 min. P.M. the Admiral made several ships signals to make more sail; at 40 min. pt. 1 he made the signal for the rear division to make more sail and the centre to close; at 2 the Ville de Paris fired several shot at our ships; at 10 min. pt. 2 began to engage; observed the Solebay a long way astern and very near the shore; at 20 min. pt. 2 she appeared to be aground, and one of the enemy's ships firing at her; ½ pt. 3 our van began to anchor in line ahead; the enemy kept a very smart fire at the rear and some of the sternmost of the centre of our fleet; at 5 came to anchor and veered away 2 cables before the ship brought up; the South point of St. Kitts bearing S.E. and Basse Terre Town N.W. and N.; at 5 min. pt. 5 discontinued the engagement; at about 7 saw the Solebay on fire; kept clear for action all night, and saw the French fleet as they wore, under the rear of our fleet, come to the wind on the larboard tack and stand to the southward; moderate and clear. Upon sounding found we had 150 fathoms; A.M. at 5 began to weigh, but having such very deep water, and the enemy's fleet standing in with a press of sail, were obliged to cut the cable, by which we lost the small bower anchor and 2 cables, with one 8-inch and one 9-inch hawsers, which were bent for springs. Employed working to windward; at 50 minutes past 8 the Admiral made the signal to engage, and began to engage accordingly;

¾ pt. 9 the Admiral sent an order for us to keep under way in the rear of the fleet; at 50 minutes past 10 he sent an order for us to anchor so as to assist the Centaur; at 55 min. pt. 10 discontinued the engagement; the Admiral made the signal for all flag officers; ½ pt. 11 Captain Coffin came on board with an order for us to continue under sail; made and shortened sail occasionally.

Sunday, 27*th*.—At anchor in Basse Terre Road, St. Kitts.—P.M. at 25 min. pt. 1 received an order from the Admiral to anchor upon the Prudent's larboard quarter; came to with the best bower in 15 fathoms and veered away to ⅔rds of a cable; ½ pt. 2 the enemy's fleet stood in in a line, and began to engage the rear of our fleet; ¾ pt. 3 discontinued the engagement; fresh breezes and clear; the enemy consisted of 29 sail of the line and 3 frigates; at 5 the Admiral made several ships signals for lieutenants and sundry other signals at different times; A.M. at 25 minutes past 9 the Admiral hoisted a Union Jack at the maintop masthead and a red pendant at the mizentop masthead, private signals; 55 min. pt. 11 the Admiral made the Sybille's, Lizard's, Convert's, and La Fortunée's signals to get under way and come to him; moderate and hazy weather.

Monday, 28*th*.—P.M. fresh breezes and squally with rain at times; at 3 the Admiral made the signal for all lieutenants; 40 min. past 10 the van of the enemy's fleet wore and brought too; A.M. fresh breezes and cloudy weather; at daylight saw the enemy's fleet to the southward; at 7 the Admiral made the signal for the 69th Regiment to prepare to disembark; at 10 the Commodore and Alcide got under weigh; the enemy's fleet bore S.W. and S. 3 or 4 miles, lying to with their heads to the northward; at 10 our frigates anchored in shore to land the troops; ½ pt. 10 the Prince George got under way; $\frac{3}{4}$ pt. 10 the St. Albans got under way; the Admiral made several ships signals and sundry other signals occasionally. At noon fresh breezes and cloudy.

Tuesday, 29*th*.—At anchor in Basse Terre Road, St. Kitts.—P.M. fresh breezes and cloudy, the Admiral made the signal for the ships under way to anchor, which the Commodore repeatd; at 1 observed the party of troops which was landed engaged with a party of the enemy's on Salt-Pans-Hill; at 9 struck the main topmast, got down the cap and got down the mizen topmast and yard, and got others up; A.M. at 1 saw the French fleet tack and stand to the southward; at 4 they stood in, and at 6 they tacked and stood off; our frigates in shore firing and several parties of the enemies troops drawn up in different places; employed knotting and splicing the rigging and filling salt water in the hold; sailmakers employ'd repairing sails.

Wednesday, 30*th*.—P.M. fresh breezes and clear; observed the frigates shifting their berths and preparing to receive the troops on board; at 3 the Admiral made the signal for all lieutenants; at 6 the troops embarked again on board the frigates; at 6 the van of the French fleet bore S.S.W. standing to the southward. Departed this life William Chapman (S.); employed fishing the main mast; A.M. fresh breezes and clear; $\frac{1}{2}$ pt. 5 the French fleet in the S.E. made the usual signal and tacked; punished John Chard (S.) for insolence; at 7 the French fleet in a line standing for the Van of our fleet; 40 min. past 10 the Adm. made the signal to engage; a few of our ships fired; at 50 min. past 10 ceased firing; at 55 min. past 10 the Admiral made the signal to annul the Commodore getting under sail; 25 min. pt. 11 he made the signal to engage; the French Van upon our firing edged away, and the whole fleet wore as they came near, and stood out upon the other tack.

Thursday, 31st.—In anchor in Basse Terre Road, St. Kitts.—Fresh breezes and cloudy with showers; P.M. ½ pt. 2 the Adm. made the Drake's sig. to come within hail; at 8 squally with rain; at 10 unbt. the mizen topsail and bent the old one; A.M. at daylight observed the French fleet much scattered, and at ½ pt. 9 they tacked and stood off in line ahead; at 11 the Admiral made our signal for a lieutenant; received some paper cartridges; observed a small man of war come to an anchor in the fleet.

February, 1782. *Friday, 1st.*—P.M. fresh gales and hazy, with hard squalls at times; at 4 the centre of the French fleet S.S.W. about 4 miles, standing in shore; ½ pt. 5 they wore, one of them standing towards Old Roads; found the small man of war which had join'd the fleet to be the Tisiphone fire-ship; A.M. fresh gales and squally with rain at times; at 6 saw part of the French fleet in the S.W.; at 8 counted from the masthead 27 sail of them; his Majesty's sloop Jane in shore hoisted French colours and fired a gun at a schooner; the Admiral made the Jane's signal to get under way, which she did and fired several shot at the schooner; sailmakers employed mending sails, &c.

Saturday, 2nd.—At anchor in Basse Terre Road, St. Kitts.—P.M. fresh breezes and squally with rain; at 6 the Convert and La Fortunée with the troops on board got under way and stood to the southward; the centre of the French fleet W.S.W. 4 miles, standing in; A.M. at 7 the French fleet in the offing counted 34 sail; at 10 saw a brig stand in shore from the French fleet, the Eurydice and Tisiphone in chace of her; the chace too near the shore, the Admiral made the signal for the ships to rejoin.

Sunday, 3rd.—P M. fresh breezes and clear; ½ pt.

2 the French fleet tacked and stood off; at 5 the Admiral made the signal for all lieutenants; A.M. at sunrise counted 17 sail of the French fleet from the masthead, 12 of whom were to the southward and the rest to the northward; ½ past 8 the Admiral made the signal for all midshipmen; received on board 4 casks of brandy, 3 of wine, 8 jars of oil, 2 of raisins, being our quota of the schooner prize; at 10, the weather clearing up, saw the rest of the enemy's fleet; got under weigh H.M. ship Champion.

Monday, 4th.—At anchor in Basse Terre Road, St. Kitts.—First moderate and hazy with squalls and showers at times, latter part moderate and clear; P.M. at 1 the Admiral made the signal for all lieutenants and for the state and condition of the ships; at 8 got down the wounded fore topmast and got another up; A.M. at 6 punished Thomas Harwood (S.) for theft; at sunrise saw 7 of the French fleet from the deck and 24 from the masthead, the centre bearing So. standing to the northward; at 7 the Admiral made our signal for a midshipman; ¼ pt. 9 beat to quarters, two of the enemy's ships standing in very near our rear; 35 minutes past 9 they wore, being little more than half gun shot; at noon the French fleet standing in from the southwards.

Tuesday, 5th.—P.M. fresh breezes and clear; ½ pt. 4 the Admiral made the signal for all lieutenants; ½ pt. 5 he made the parole signal a flag half red half white at the foretop masthead; A.M., at sunrise the French fleet in the S.W.; counted from the masthead 32 sail and 2 ships and 6 vessels in the N.W.; at 7 loosed courses, topsails, jib and staysails to air, washed the lower gun deck, &c.

Wednesday, 6th.—At anchor in Basse Terre Road, St. Kitts.—P.M. fresh gales and clear; at daylight counted 32 sail of the French fleet, 6 sloops and 3 brigs; ½ pt. 5 the Admiral made the parole signal a flag half blue half yellow at the foretop masthead; the French fleet close in tacked and stood to the southward; A.M. fresh gales and hazy, with showers at times; at daylight the French fleet standing in; counted 32 square-rigged vessels; at 7 the Admiral made the Lizard's signal to speak a strange sail in the S.E.; a ship standing in with a signal of distress and English colours hoisted; at 8 the French fleet tacked and stood out; at 9 the Champion, Lizard, Eurydice and Tisiphone got under way and came to an anchor close in with the Basse Terre.

Thursday, 7th.—P.M. fresh gales and squally with showers; the Champion, Lizard, Eurydice and Tisiphone got under weigh from Basse Terre, each with a ship in tow; at 4 the Champion and Tisiphone cast off their tow and anchored; the Eurydice and Lizard anchored with their ships in tow; ½ pt. 5 the French fleet wore and stood to the southward; the Admiral made the parole signal a flag half yellow half blue at the foretop masthead; A.M. fresh breezes and cloudy; at 6 counted 28 sail of the enemy's fleet standing in; at 10 the Admiral made the signal for all cruizers; washed the lower gun deck; the French fleet close in with Nevis; ½ pt. 11 the Admiral made the signal to prepare for action; two of the enemy's ships took a schooner working into the Narrows.

Friday, 8th.—At anchor in Basse Terre Road, St. Kitts.—Fresh breezes and clear; P.M. ½ pt. 5 the Admiral made the parole signal a flag half white half blue at ye foretop masthead; A.M. at daylight counted 22 sail of the French fleet from the masthead, the Eurydice, Champion and Tisiphone under way standing for the Narrows; the Admiral made the signal to recall the ships in the S.E., the Lizard being at an anchor far to leeward and an 80-gun ship of the enemy's standing for her; the Admiral made her signal to weigh and come nearer him, and soon after her signal to anchor; the French ship bore away towards Old Roads; $\frac{3}{4}$ pt. 7 beat to quarters; the enemy's fleet standing in, in line ahead; at 9 the headmost of the enemy's van wore, and the rest of the fleet did the same as they.

Saturday, 9th.—P.M. fresh breezes and clear; the Admiral made the signal for all midshipmen; $\frac{1}{2}$ pt. 5 he made the parole signal a flag half white half red at the foretop masthead; down topsail yards; A.M. moderate and hazy; sailed the Tisiphone, the Champion and Eurydice, standing in for the Narrows; at daylight the enemies fleet off Nevis Point standing in; at 6 the Admiral made the signal to recall the ships in the S.E.; at 7 the Lizard went to leeward and hoisted a French ensign several times, which the Admiral answered; punished Thomas Harwood (S.) for committing a robbery; at 8 got up topsail yards; loos'd topsails and small sails to air; at 10, one of the enemy's frigates, 5 brigs and several sloops and schooners passed to leeward; at noon the enemies fleet 22 line-of-battle ships, lying to about 2 miles from our ships.

Sunday, 10th.—At anchor in Basse Terre Road, St. Kitts.—P.M. fresh breezes and hazy; at 20 min. P.M. the French fleet wore and stood to the southward; at sunset the Admiral made the parole signal a flag half red half yellow at the foretop masthead; counted 20 ships of the enemy's fleet; down topsail yards; A.M. moderate and cloudy; at 8 up topsail yards, counted 24 sail of the enemy's fleet; at 9 the Admiral made the signal to recall the ships cruizing in the S.E., and our signal for a midshipman; at 10, one of the enemy's ships stood in with her mizentopsail aback, and sent a launch on board the leeward most vessel which had been brought out of Basse Terre Road and set her on fire; the French ship wore and stood for the enemy's fleet; observed a flag of truce go on board the Ville de Paris from the Barfleur.

Monday, 11*th*.—At anchor in Basse Terre Road, St. Kitts.—P.M. fresh breezes and cloudy; mustered the ship's company; received on board 5,000 weight of yams in lieu of bread; at sunset the Admiral made the parole signal a flag half yellow half blue at the foretop masthead; the French fleet tacked and stood off; observed a French brig towing in the flag of truce; A.M. moderate and clear; unbent the mizen topsail, repaired it and bent it again; at sunrise the French fleet in sight from the masthead bearing S.S.E.; loosed sails to dry; at noon the French fleet extended some considerable distance; they wore and stood off; our frigates warping the hospital ship to windward.

Tuesday, 12*th*.—P.M. moderate and clear; a French line-of-battle ship passed our fleet, with her maintop mast down, standing for Old Roads; at 3 the French line-of-battle ship which passed our fleet made sail to leeward, after having brought to some time in Old Roads; at sunset the Admiral made the parole signal a flag half red half white at the foretop masthead; at 6 the French fleet standing in bearing S. and E.; A.M. moderate and cloudy; at 7 saw 16 sail of the enemy's fleet from the masthead; a small schooner standing in from the southward; the Admiral made the Champion signal to chace her, and soon after he made the signal for her to leave off chace to the southward and chace to the N.W.; at noon 24 sail of the French fleet in the offing; observed a frigate standing in for Old Roads.

Wednesday, 13*th*.—At anchor in Basse Terre Road, St. Kitts.—Moderate and clear; P.M. the

Lizard went to leeward to communicate by signal with Brimstone Hill; ½ pt. 3, on seeing 3 French line-of-battle ships and a frigate standing in to endeavour to cut off the Lizard, the Admiral made the Centaur's, Belliqueux's, Resolution's, Prudent's, and our signals to prepare for battle; one of the French line-of-battle ships fired a shot at the Lizard, but it did not reach; they wore and stood off; A.M. at 6 the Champion weighed and made the signal for 2 strange sails in the N.E.; counted 26 sail of the enemy's fleet; at 7 the Lizard got under way and made signals to Brimstone Hill; several ships appeared in sight from the eastward and join'd the French fleet; up topsail yards; at 8 counted 41 sail of the enemies fleet from the masthead; the Admiral made our signal for a lieutenant; between 10 and 11 heard the report of several guns; at noon the French fleet standing in; arrived the Gros Islet.

Thursday, 14*th*.—P.M. fresh breezes and clear; ½ pt. some frigates appearing coming thro' the Narrows, several of the French ships made sail to cut them off; the Admiral made the signal to prepare for battle; arrived H.M. ship Triton and the Blast and Salamander (fireships); the French ships tacked and joined the fleet again; at 40 min. pt. 5 the Admiral made the signal for all flag officers; heard that Brimstone Hill had capitulated at 10 o'clock this morning; the Admiral made the parole signal a flag half white half blue at the fore topgallant masthead; down topsail yards; A.M. at daylight counted 30 sail of the enemies fleet bearing S.E.; at 8 observed the French fleet come to an anchor off Nevis Point, and very far out; at 11 the Admiral made the signal for all lieutenants; at noon some of the French ships drove off the Bank and are working up.

Friday, 15*th*.—At anchor in Basse Terre Road, St. Kitts.—P.M. moderate and clear; at 3 the Admiral made the signal for the ships to weigh their stream anchors and hoist their long-boats in; at 4 the Admiral made the signal for all lieutenants; hove in some of the cable and cast off the springs, &c.; at sunset the Admiral made the parole signal a flag half red half yellow at the foretop masthead; at 9 a lieutenant attended the Admiral for orders; at 11 cut the best bower cable by order; set the jib and cast to the southward; the ships cut in succession and formed the line ahead, the Alfred leading under single-reef top; at 12 Old Road N.N.W.; made and shortened sail occasionally; A.M. squally wear.; counted 27 sail in company; employed stowing the anchors and fixing preventer shrouds for the foremast; departed this life William Head (M.); ½ pt. 11, the Lizard made sail to leeward and parted company; made and shortened sail occasionally; in company with the Admiral and fleet.

Saturday, 16*th*.—P.M. moderate and clear; at 8 haul'd up the larboard cluegarnet of the foresail; hauled aft the larboard fore sheet, made and shortened sail occasionally; A.M. moderate and cloudy; at 4 punished Robt. Cahail (S.) for neglect; ¼ pt. 5 hauled up the lee cluegarnet of the foresail; at 6 hauled aft the fore sheet; at 8 the Admiral made the signal for the state and condition of the ships; made and shortened sail occasionally; at noon, moderate and cloudy, the Admiral made sundry signals occasionally. In company with the Admiral and fleet.

Sunday, 17*th*.—P.M. little wind and clear; ½ pt. 2 the Admiral made the signal for all flag officers; made and shortened sail occasionally; A.M. little wind with showers at times; at 4 a breeze sprung up; the fleet much scattered; loosed topsails, and small sails to air; made and shortened sail occasionally; at noon light airs and clear, in company with the Admiral and fleet.

Monday, 18th.—Moderate and clear; P.M. loosed topsails to dry; at 8 the Admiral made the signal to tack; at 10 tacked, made and shortened sail occasionally; A.M. little wind and clear; ½ pt. 6 brought to, lowered the main topsail to repair; made and shortened sail occasionally. At noon in company with the Admiral and fleet.

Tuesday, 19th.—P.M. moderate and clear; at 5 the Admiral made the signal for the fleet to close; the Commodore made the signal for his division to make more sail; ½ pt. 5 the Admiral made the Eurydice's signal to keep ahead during the night; made and shortened sail occasionally; A.M. fresh breezes and clear; ¾ pt. 5 the Admiral made the signal for the fleet to close; ½ past 6 the Pegasus made the private signal and joined the fleet; ¼ pt. 7 the Admiral brought to and spoke the Pegasus; at 9 he made the signal to form the line ahead one cable's length asunder, and the second in command to lead; at 10 he made the signal for the line of bearing S.S.E. and N.N.W. one cable's length asunder; made and shortened sail occasionally; at noon moderate and clear. In company with the Admiral and fleet.

Wednesday, 20th.—At anchor in St. John's Road, Antigua.—P.M. fresh breezes and squally; ½ pt. 1 the Admiral made the signal to bring to, the rear first; ½ pt. 3 the Admiral made the signal to alter the line of bearing to N.N.E. and S.S.W., and the signal to anchor; at 5 fresh breezes and cloudy; made and shortened sail occasionally; ½ pt. 6 came to anchor in St. John's Road in 11 fathoms water, in company with the Admiral and fleet; Ship's-stern[1] S. ½ E., Sister Islands N.E. and E., and the Warrington E. ½ S.; A.M. fresh breezes and clear; the Admiral made the signal for all lieutenants; found here H.M. ship La Couvert and La Fortunée, Sybille, and several other small vessels; at noon sail'd La Fortunée and Pegasus.

LORD ROBERT MANNERS TO HIS BROTHER [THE DUKE OF RUTLAND].

The three following letters from Lord Robert Manners are printed together here, in order to complete the papers relating to the operations at St. Kitts. They are quoted from the 'Fourteenth Report of the Historical MSS. Commission, Apdendix, Part I.'

8th of February, 1782.—The Resolution, St. Kitts.—I set down to write to you, though the signal is now flying to prepare for battle. The enemy consist of twenty-nine sail of the line and three 50-gun ships standing in for us. Therefore you must not expect a long letter or a very correct account, as I am frequently looking out to observe their progress. They have already made three attacks upon us without success, and, I believe, have received infinitely more damage than they have done us. One of their attacks was pretty severe, and fell mostly on our rear; we came off very well in point of men, but are much cut in the masts and rigging, having our bowsprit, all our lower masts, all our top masts, and all our top gallant masts wounded, owing to our peculiar situation when the French made the attack, which I have not time at present to describe; all I

[1] 'The Ship-stern is "a small, flat-topped, rocky islet," a cable westward of Goat Hill Point on the west side of Antigua, so called because its own west side has somewhat that appearance.'—*West India Pilot*, ii. 95.

have to say is that if our reinforcement should precede that of the French we shall do very well, if not I cannot guess the consequences.

You know, I suppose, that though the citadel on Brimstone Hill still holds out, the rest of the island remains in possession of the French, which makes our situation not so tenable as it would be were we further in shore, which we cannot be, on account of the batteries the French may erect, without being exposed; an attempt, indeed, was made by the troops to take possession of the heights, but without effect, and General Prescott, thinking it out of his power to throw any succours into Brimstone Hill, or to take possession of any post which would be tenable, returned a week ago with the troops to Antigua. Sir Samuel Hood seems determined that we shall see the event of the business, expecting, I believe—what I fear he will be mistaken in—a reinforcement previous to De Grasse's. I understand the French commanding officers are all at variance. De Grasse is not for risking his squadron, probably wishing to preserve it for the more important conquest of Jamaica. The Marquis de Bouillé declares he will not give the island up, though De Grasse should leave him, and Bougainville sides with De Bouillé. The taking possession of this road was well judged, well conducted, and well executed, though indeed the French had an opportunity—which they missed—of bringing our rear to a very severe account. The van and centre divisions brought to an anchor under the fire of the rear, which was engaged with the enemy's centre, and then, the centre being at an anchor and properly placed, covered us while we anchored, making, I think, the most masterly manœuvre I ever saw.

With the utmost concern I must inform you of an event which will hurt you much, I am sure, which is the loss of poor Brown;[1] he went in the long-boat in company with other ships' boats to bring out a vessel for the reception of our wounded men some days after the action, and has never returned, nor have I had the least tidings of him or the boat; another long-boat was lost, but her people are saved. There were in our boat ten of the best men in the ship, which, with him, has given me most inexpressible concern. I had a very sincere regard for him. There is but one ray of hope, in his being taken by some one of the enemy's small vessels, of which there are a good many cruising under the land, and which might have escaped us. I have permission, and intend to send a flag of truce to the Marquis de Bouillé to inquire if such a capture has been made, but I do not flatter myself much with hopes.

The constant sight of the enemy has made them quite familiar to us, and though at least once a day they form in such a position as to make it appear they are going to attack us, yet when they come near gunshot they always tack, and stand from our fleet. If they mean by this to harass us they are quite mistaken, as we have always time to make our meals in the twenty-four hours, but it must fatigue them exceedingly, the currents constantly obliging them to carry a great deal of sail to keep their station, and we have the satisfaction to observe them carrying away something daily, especially those ships which appear to have suffered in the action. You know we are at anchor and the French under sail. I have put this on paper to give you some

[1] Poor Brown turned out to be safe after all. He and his boat's crew were taken prisoners and carried to St. Eustatius. There are several Browns—the surgeon, his servant, and four seamen—on the pay-books of the Resolution. Lord R. Manners was, no doubt, speaking of the surgeon, who had gone to choose a hospital ship.

little idea of our situation; you must not suppose it accurate. The intention of the enemy seems to be an attack on our rear. I have put down the names of the ships which are likely to sustain it, also the three Admiral's ships. The enemy still keep the appearance of an inclination for an attack this evening, therefore I will finish this letter and send it on board the vessel which is to sail to-night if she can get clear. The Admiral only to-day signified his intentions of sending his despatches home, or you should have heard more particulars, which you shall the first opportunity. *Rough plan.*

LORD ROBERT MANNERS TO HIS BROTHER [THE DUKE OF RUTLAND].

22nd of February, 1782.—St. John's Road, Antigua.—My last letter informed you of our situation at St. Kitts. The very day after we perceived an alteration in the garrison, and they apprised us by signals appointed that many of their works were destroyed, and that by two batteries the enemy had last erected they had lost many men. Two days after we had the same unpleasant signal repeated, on which the Admiral sent an officer to endeavour to get into the hill to learn more particularly their situation, but could not effect it, and on the 15th of February a flag of truce came off to say it had capitulated, having two very large breaches in the wall, their magazines of rum and provisions utterly destroyed by shells, and the different works so defaced and damaged as not to be any longer tenable. Few situations could have been more unpleasing than ours—to see an island surrender in our sight without having it in our power to afford any relief beside that of passively remaining and keeping possession of our ground in sight of it. However,[1] we had the satisfaction of reflecting that every exertion which it lay in our power to make had not been neglected. Had the troops we carried from Antigua been sufficient to have thrown themselves into the hill, in all probability the French would have abandoned their design, in which case I think it would have been one of the most brilliant events [of] this war. After the surrender of the island it became highly necessary for us to take some immediate steps for our own safety, as then the manœuvres of the enemy both by sea and land indicated a very severe attack, had they collected their whole force, which consisted of thirty-four sail of the line and thirteen small vessels, which we imagined to be fireships, and were anchored within four or five miles of us, to windward; on shore they were beginning to raise bomb batteries, and the Marquis de Bouillé, with 3,000 men, was marching to operate against us from that quarter. The Admiral, having some intimation of this, did not, you may imagine, hesitate long what steps he should take, therefore summoned his captains and told them he should cut his cables at eleven o'clock that night without making any signal, and, having regulated our watches accordingly, we each cut our cables at the same precise moment of time, and sailed out in a line with so little noise or confusion that the enemy did not miss us for four hours after. Nothing could have been more fortunately executed, as not one accident happened from it.

Taking the whole in one light, though not successful in the point we aimed at, nevertheless it was well conducted, and has given the enemy a pretty

[1] Lord Robert Manners meant to say, 'no exertion has been neglected.'

severe check, and if you give him half the credit the enemy does, Sir Samuel Hood will stand very high in the public estimation. Their sea officers say it was a bold and well-conducted attempt, but they were sure our getting possession of Basse Terre Road could be of no consequence, as they knew we had not troops sufficient to relieve the place. However, they confess they cannot keep the line of battle with that precision we do, and manœuvre with so much sail out without the danger of running aboard each other. The Marquis de Bouillé, St. Simon, and the land officers set no bounds to their praises; they speak in the highest terms of our manœuvres, and contrasting them with their own, draw a comparison not very flattering to the latter; but I must tell you they are [at] variance with De Grasse, for De Grasse sent to the M. de Bouillé, two days before the surrender, to say that if the island did not surrender by that day week he would positively leave it, whether he chose to embark or not. I wish it had held out long enough for them to have put his resolution in practice.

Comte Dillon, who is appointed Governor of St. Kitts, told an officer of the navy who was sent with a flag of truce by Sir Samuel Hood, that it was not necessary to keep their intentions any longer secret, that Barbadoes and Antigua were the next objects, then Jamaica, and lastly New York, and then they will consent to make peace; and in my conscience I believe they intend all this, as we have just received accounts of the arrival of the remainder of the Marquis de Vaudreuil's squadron, which, together with four Spanish men-of-war also arrived, make their fleet, now lying within twelve leagues of us, forty-four sail of the line, a most astonishing fleet, and out of those only five of sixty-four guns; ours consists of twenty-two of the line, and we are taught to expect

Sir George Rodney with a large reinforcement, but have as yet heard nothing to be depended upon.

I have not got Brown yet, but the Comte de Grasse has promised he would send him and all my people and long-boat, and I believe would have done it had we remained a day longer in Basse Terre Road. We are on the point of leaving this place to proceed to Barbadoes—as I imagine—to join our reinforcement. The inhabitants petition Sir Samuel very much to stay here with the squadron, which he does not think proper to do for the above-mentioned reason.

LORD ROBERT MANNERS TO [THE DUKE OF RUTLAND].

10th of March, 1782.—The Resolution, St. Lucia.—Sir George Rodney is arrived with a force which gives a new face to the affairs of this country; not that I mean the lost islands will be recovered, but I think the few remaining Windward Islands are safe, and that the designs of the enemy on Jamaica will be frustrated. The very defenceless state of all our islands through the want of troops will always oblige him to act on the defensive, as no island is safe but the one we are immediately protecting; at least it was the case before the arrival of Sir George and his reinforcement.

The Resolution is ordered to sea this morning, and not in the most pleasant condition, being entirely destitute of stores, and all our rigging condemned as unserviceable. To say the truth, she herself complains a little. I am administering to her the most salutary and efficacious remedies that can be applied in this country, and there is soon to be a consultation of carpenters upon her, as it is generally supposed a change of climate will be found the only means of restoring her health, which has been lately very much impaired; and as her disorder is chiefly a violent relaxation in all her parts, so as to admit of the free ingress and egress of water—the reverse of a diabetes—I opine a northern climate is the most proper to brace her up and restore many of her faculties, which she has now, I grieve to say, entirely lost.

Next month the ship will have been three years coppered and out of dock, which is the usual time of their service; and from the loss of the Terrible, and the very bad state of the ships of the same standing, it is probable they will go home at nearly the same time. It is remarked that copper-bottom ships, when they once begin to show their defects, drop all at once, which is the case of the Invincible, who is now in as bad a state as the Terrible was, and several others, which they are afraid even to trust home.

I heard with much concern of the loss you met with at Brookes', but I trust it was not to the extent of what I heard.

If Sir George Rodney chooses to risk the marines of the fleet, I think he may retake Montserrat or some such island, but he is not strong enough in troops to recapture St. Kitts or Granada, or any of the more important islands, without leaving some of our own in the power of the enemy. The French convoy is not yet arrived at Martinique, as I wrote you word of before, so that they have now but thirty-six sail of the line, but the rest are expected very soon. I want much to hear from England how you take the loss of St. Kitts and the settlements of Demerara and the rest on the main.

Brown is returned home with all my people from St. Eustatius, from whence they were sent by the Comte de Grasse, who very politely lamented the loss of the boat, as it prevented him from sending them immediately, and in the same state in which they were taken.

SIR SAMUEL HOOD'S JOURNAL.

Jan. (*Friday*, 25*th*), 1782.—Extremes of Nevis Point, Rodondo and Montserrat.—Moderate breezes and cloudy weather; 14 min. past noon, made the Fortunée's signal for her captain; at same time made the Russell's signal for a lieutenant; 12 m. past 1 P.M. made the Prince William's signal for her captain; ½ past 1 do. answered the Shrewsbury's signal for a sail in the S. East; 55 min. past 1 do. Rear-Admiral Drake made the Alcide's signal for being out of her station, and at 25 min. past 2 do. he made the Ajax's signal for being out of her station; at 3 do. I made the Alfred and St. Alban's signals to change stations in the line; 26 min. past do. made the Jane, Drake, Gros Islet, and Expedition's signal for their commanders; 16 min. past 4 do. answered the Champion's signal for 3 sail in the N.E.; 20 min. past do. Rear-Admiral Drake made the signal for his division to close; 11 min. past 5 I made the Nymphe's signal for her captain; ¾ past 5 came into the fleet a large French cutter, prize to the Lizard and Couvert; ½ past 5 do. the Commodore made the signal for his division to close; Rear-Admiral Drake made the Intrepid's and Ajax's signals for being out of their stations; made the Fortunée's signal for a lieutenant; brought to; at 6 do. answered the Princesa's and Centaur's signals for seeing a fleet; at 8 do. made the signal to make sail after lying by; ½ past 9 do. made the signal to tack; at 10 saw 20 strange vessels in the N.W., which proved to be the French fleet; ½ past 1 A.M. observed them to tack and stand to the northward; at 2 do. tacked ship, the extremes of Nevis from N.*b*.W., to N.W., the headmost of the French fleet N.W.*b*.N., and the sternmost, W.*b*.S.; made and shortened sail occasionally; ¾ past 5 A.M. answered the Sybille's signal for seeing a sail in the S.E.; at do. made the signal to tack, saw several flashes of guns on the weather quarter; at 6 tacked, as did the fleet, shortened sail and brought to; Rodondo, N.E. ½ E., distance 4 leagues; 11 min. past 6 A.M. made the signal for a line of battle ahead at one cable's length asunder; 16 min. past 6 do. made the L'Espion's signal to come within hail; Rear-Admiral Drake made the signal for his division to make more sail; at do. I made the Fortunée's signal for her captain; 24 min. past 7 do. Rear-Admiral Drake made the signal for the St. Alban's to close in the line, at the same time the Centaur made the signal for a strange sail in the N.E.; ¾ past 7 do. I made the signal for the Van to fill; at 3 do. made the St. Alban's signal to make more sail; 14 min. past 8 do. made the leading ship's signal to alter her course two points to port; 28 min. past 8 do. made the Shrewsbury's signal for being out of her station; at 9 do. made the Couvert's signal for her captain; at 8 min. past 9 do. made the leading ship's signal to alter her course three points to starboard; 15 min. past 9 made the Ajax's signal for being out of her station; 20 min. past 9 do. made the Couvert's signal to come within hail; 23 min. past 9 do. made the leading ship's signal to alter her course two points to port; 25 min. past 9 made the signal for the rear of the fleet to bring too, and the Couvert's signal for her captain; 42 min. past 10 made the signal for the Van ships to make more sail; 52 min. past 10 do. made signal for the leading ships when in a line to hoist, lower, set, or haul up any sail after the Commander-in-Chief; 5 minutes past

11 made the signal for the rear to close with the centre; 41 min. past 11 do. made the Belliqueux's signal to make more sail; 46 min. past 11 made the signal to prepare to anchor in a line of battle; the body of the French fleet S.W.*b*.W. 4 or 5 miles (twenty-nine sail of which of the line); at 12 made the Couvert's signal for her captain.

Jan. (*Saturday*, 26*th*), 1782.—Basse Terre Road, St. Christopher's.—Moderate and clear weather; 26 min. past noon made the signal for the leading ship to alter her course to starboard; 5 min. past 1 P.M. Rear-Admiral Drake made the signal for his division to close; 30 min. past 1 do. I made the signal for the rear to close the centre; 41 min. past 1 do. repeated the above signal; 52 min. past 1 do. made the Monarch's signal to make more sail; 57 min. past 1 do. made the Alfred's signal to make more sail; 5 min. past 2 do. made the Montagu's signal to make more sail; at 6 min. past 2 do. the enemy began to engage our rear, who immediately returned their fire; ½ past 2 do. the Barfleur opened her fire upon the enemy; 49 min. past 2 do. furled topgallant sails and shortened sail, and laid the main and mizen topsails to the mast; 58 min. past 2 filled the topsails; 5 min. past 3 do. made the Shrewsbury's signal for being out of her station; 12 min. past 3 do. made the Fortunée's signal for her captain; 58 min. past 3 the Van of the enemy's fleet wore, when we ceased firing, our rear still in action; at 3 min. past 4 do. came to an anchor in Basseterre Road, with the small bower in 20 fathom water, the west point of St. Kitts W.N.W., James Fort N.W., and Frigate Bay S. by E. ½ E. about 3 miles, veered too half a cable on the spring; 40 min. past 4 do. the Barfleur opened her fire again on the enemy's fleet; 53 min. past 4 do. hauled down the signal for the line; 26 min. past 5 do. both fleets ceased firing, hoisted out the boats, and employed repairing the damages sustained in action; saw the Solebay on fire off Nevis Point, she having got aground coming in with the fleet; A.M. at 6 saw the French fleet bearing S.S.E. distant 7 or 8 miles; at 7 do. several of our fleet under way getting into their stations in the line, the enemy then in a line of battle ahead twenty-nine sail, standing towards the Van of our fleet; at 8 A.M. got the stream anchor and cable out on the larboard quarter for a spring; 42 min. past 8 do. I made the signal for battle; 43 min. past 8 do. the Van of both fleets began to engage; 53 min. past 8 do. the Barfleur opened her fire on the enemy; 40 min. past 10 the Barfleur ceased firing, and at 50 min. past 10 do. the firing ceased on both sides; at same time I made the signal for all flag officers; 10 min. past 11 do. made the Monarch's, Centaur's, Belliqueux's, and Resolution's signal for captains; employed repairing the damages sustained in action.

HOOD TO STEPHENS.

Barfleur, at Sea, 22nd of February, 1782.

Sir:—Herewith you will receive duplicates of my last letters by the Tisiphone.

From the very strong assurances Governor Shirley gave me of Brimstone Hill being in a state of the most perfect security, and from the spirited and encouraging message sent by General Frazer to General Prescott on the 24th of last month, I had not the smallest doubt of relieving the island after I got possession of the enemy's anchorage in Basseterre Road. And the Governor having expressed a wish for an able sea officer, and a few seamen, I sent Captain Curgenven and Lieutenant

Hare (late of the Solebay), who were eager volunteers, with thirty men, in two boats, to endeavour to throw themselves into the garrison in the night. The oars were muffled, and every precaution used that not the least noise should be made to give an alarm, but upon putting the boats' sterns to the shore, volley after volley of musketry were fired at them, and they were obliged to return. Two nights after, the man I first sent upon the Hill, and whom Captain Curgenven took with him, thought he could make his way *alone* to the garrison; he made the trial in a small canoe, but was forced to return, having been fired at from every part he attempted to land. On the same evening Lieutenant Fayhie, of the Russell, was put on shore in Red Flag Bay, on the north side of the island (his father is Judge of the Admiralty, was upon the Hill, and whose estate is close to the foot of it). Mr. Fayhie, knowing every accessible path to the Hill, was sanguine in his hopes of being able to reach the garrison, but after waiting two nights found it impossible, and returned.

Upon the signals being made from the Hill on the 8th that the enemy's batteries had been successful in damaging the works and buildings, that the garrison was reduced and short of ordnance stores, I was eager to make further trials to get an officer upon the Hill, and Captain Curgenven again offering his service, as well as Captain Bourne of the Marines, I sent them away that evening in a small boat, towed by another, near the place they expected to land; and after being on shore ten minutes Captain Curgenven returned and ordered the boats on board, but neither succeeded in reaching the garrison, and both were made prisoners in different places.

About the time these officers left the Barfleur, Lieutenant Fayhie was again landed on the north side of the island, being desirous of making another trial from his father's estate, but as he is not yet returned, and I have heard nothing from him, I conclude he was taken prisoner.

I was extremely desirous of getting an officer into the garrison, just to say I was confident the Count de Grasse was weary of his situation, and as the Marquis de Bouillé was destroying every fort and magazine at Basseterre, and blew up their very foundations, I was persuaded he despaired of success, and that if the Hill could hold out ten days longer the island must be saved.

But I am much concerned to say that Captain Robinson, of the 15th Regiment, in the evening of the 13th, came on board the Barfleur to inquire for General Prescott, being charged with a letter for him from Governor Shirley and General Frazer, acquainting him of their having surrendered the garrison to the arms of the French king that morning.

The information I got from Captain Robinson is as follows: that he was sent to Monsieur St. Simon at seven in the evening of the 12th, to propose a cessation of arms; at the same hour another officer was sent on the same errand to the Marquis de Bouillé, and so eager was the Marquis to get possession of the Hill that he granted *all* that was asked, and the terms were agreed to at his (Captain Robinson's) return to the garrison at midnight. I inquired if no article was stipulated for my being made acquainted with the state of the garrison before the surrender took place, and to my great surprise was answered in the *negative.*

On the 14th the enemy's fleet anchored off Nevis, consisting of the Ville de Paris, six ships of eighty guns, twenty-three of seventy-four, and four of sixty-four. One sixty-four was at Old Road and another at Sandy Point; the Triomphant and Brave had joined from Europe.

Under this situation of things I had no longer any business in Basseterre Road, especially as the enemy were preparing to get guns and mortars upon a height that would annoy the ships in the van, and I left it that night, unperceived I imagine, as not one of the enemy's ships was to be seen in the morning.

With so vast a superiority against me I had nothing left to do but to endeavour to join Sir George Rodney as fast as I was able; and as it was of very great importance to the King's service that I should carry his Majesty's squadron to him in as perfect a state as possible, I judged it necessary, in order that every ship should be under sail as nearly as possible at the same *moment*, for the better preserving a compact body, to give directions for the squadron to cut, in which Rear-Admiral Drake most readily concurred, and thought highly expedient, from the expectation there was of our being attacked, the enemy's ships being not more than five miles from us, and their lights very distinctly seen.

Except Governor Shirley's letter, and the message General Prescott's officer brought from General Frazer, of the 24th of last month, I never heard a syllable from Brimstone Hill, or from *any one person in the island*; and what is still more extraordinary to tell, the garrison in all probability could not have been reduced but for the *eight* brass 24-pound cannon, *two* 13-inch brass mortars, 1,500 shells, and 6,000 24-pound cannon-balls the enemy found at the foot of the hill, which Government had sent out, and which the inhabitants of the island would not give proper assistance for getting up. For the enemy's ship with the shells was sunk, and it was with difficulty more than four or five of a day could be fished up; and L'Espion, in which were all the shells could be got from Martinique, was taken by one of my advanced frigates close under Nevis, on the morning I first appeared off the island.

I understand the terms of the surrender have been founded on the articles of capitulation agreed upon at the reduction of Dominica. This is all I am able to tell you for their Lordships' information, and I am far from meaning in the most distant manner to suggest that the garrison *could* have held out a single day longer, as I am told the works and buildings were a heap of ruins, and that no further defence could be made with the least probable prospect of success.

I anchored his Majesty's squadron in St. John's Road on the 19th after sunset, to get some flour and yams in lieu of bread; sailed again this noon to seek Sir George Rodney at Barbadoes, and get a supply of water, and I hope to find the convoy arrived to have all our wants furnished. The Fortunée and Pegasus, which I left to watch the French fleet, have this instant joined, and report that thirty-six sail of the line quitted Basseterre Road yesterday morning, with upwards of fifty sail of brigs, sloops and schooners, and steered for Martinique.

Herewith you will receive an account of the state and condition of his Majesty's squadron under my command.

I have the honour to be, Sir,
Your most obedient and most humble Servant,
SAM. HOOD.

N.B.—Since writing the above I have received the enclosed intelligence from a vessel under Imperial colours, which left Martinique on the 19th.

Endorsed.—22nd of February, 1782.
Sir Saml. Hood.

℞ 26th of March by Captain Everit.

Intelligence from the brig Hercules,
Alexander Kennedy, Master, from St. Pierre's, Martinique.
Three days out, viz. :

That two sail of the line had arrived on the 1st of February, and that there was a report that fourteen sail of Spanish ships of the line had arrived at Fort Royal; a brig that arrived three weeks since gave an account of twenty-seven sail of merchant ships, under the convoy of five frigates, had sailed from France; that part of our fleet fell in with them shortly after their sailing, and had taken part of the convoy and two frigates. The above brig was one of the convoy. The Mohawk, Brutus, Fair American, with another American privateer, were laying at Martinique. And that on last Sunday the Marseilles convoy with two frigates arrived. No accounts from Demerara.

That the French have been ever since the departure of their fleet under great apprehensions of an attack, having neither troops or ammunition to defend the island. The Marquis de Bouillé has sent orders to sell off all his household furniture, as he means to go home after the attack of Jamaica, which was intended when the Spanish reinforcement had arrived.

The above [mentioned] brig came between Guadaloupe and Montserrat, and this morning saw a very large fleet standing to the southward, and ten or twelve ships under Montserrat.

The December packet had been carried into Martinique; the despatches on board destroyed. From the surgeon of her we have gained the above intelligence, being passenger on board her to Ostend.

(Signed) JOHN STANHOPE.

HOOD TO STEPHENS.

Barfleur, at Sea, 23rd of February, 1782.

Sir:—When his Majesty's squadron under my command was without bread, I procured yams for the people to help out with the flour; and though the men were under arms from the 25th of last month to the 15th instant, they performed their duty with that cheerfulness and good humour which charmed me.

I therefore take the liberty humbly to propose to their Lordships that the yams should be a present upon this extraordinary occasion; it will show the poor fellows they are attended to, and will, I am persuaded, be productive of very happy effects.

I have the honour to be, with great truth and esteem, Sir,

Your most obedient and most humble Servant,

SAM. HOOD.

HOOD TO JACKSON.

Barfleur, Gros Islet Bay, St. Lucia, 31st of March, 1782.

My dear Sir:—As I feared, foretold, and laboured to prevent, the French armament is safe arrived in Fort Royal Bay, making Deseada, and running down between Dominica and Martinique. If I had been asking the greatest boon for myself, I could not have been more earnest in my entreaties to Sir George Rodney, so soon as I returned from the cul-de-sac on the 7th of last month, to divide his force and station one-half off Deseada, and the other off Point Salines; but he would not hear of it, said the French always made Salines Point, to the contrary of which I took the liberty of giving him two or three instances to the contrary (*sic*), and added that admitting there was the greatest probability that the expected convoy would make Salines Point, and but a bare possibility of its making Deseada, I humbly submitted whether it would not be prudent to guard against that possibility, for allow the enemy to come here fourteen sail of the line strong, you can have two squadrons of eighteen sail of the line, which will admit of four sail to play upon the transports and storeships, and still have ship for ship; and the destruction of the transports seems to me an object deserving attention. Sir George was perfectly silent to this. The February packet arrived here on the 8th, and took a brig from Bourdeaux bound to Martinique, the prisoners of which said the armament was then about to sail from Brest; and as a Dane was arrived here in twenty-nine days from Spithead, I could not help suggesting to Sir George whether the French convoy might not be daily expected. His answer was, Oh no, he was sure it would not sail before March. I gave in to the probability of it, but thought it very possible to happen otherwise; and as the greatest part of his fleet was ready for sea, I expressed my wishes in the strongest manner to be allowed to cruize off Deseada, and between that island and Dominica. After receiving two or three different orders, I went to sea on the 16th with eleven sail, Captain Cornish being added to my squadron the evening before; but I was limited from five to ten leagues to windward of Salines Point. On the next day I spoke with Captain Ford, of La Nymphe frigate from Antigua, where a ship was arrived which sailed from Spithead under convoy of the Princess Caroline on the 11th of last month, and parted company the same evening in a snowstorm; and on the 14th was spoken with by the Arethusa, and received written information from Sir Richard Pearson that he had fallen in with, just come out of Brest, fourteen sail of the line and six frigates, having under convoy 100 sail of transports and storeships. I despatched La Nymphe to Sir George Rodney without detaining her a moment. On the 20th, in the afternoon, I saw the Commander-in-Chief's flag to leeward, and at midnight I received the arrangement No. 1 for the fleets cruizing, and at the same time a private note from Sir George, to which I replied that I rejoiced most exceedingly he had been pleased to extend his ships so far to the northward, for that the Commander of the French squadron must be a madman to think of coming in sight of St. Lucia, knowing, as he must, the force of the British fleet, which would naturally be upon the look out; but at 8 A.M. on the 23rd, not more than thirty hours after I got his cruizing arrangement, he sent me the letter No. 2, which I trouble you with to show the unsteadiness of the man; and as a further proof of it he did not send Commodore Affleck and the two sixty-fours to the northward until the 26th, nor do I believe that a single frigate was stationed off Deseada—for the first intelligence Sir George received of the arrival of the French armament in Fort Royal Bay, on the 20th, was by an officer (English) who came from Martinique in a cartel, and got to Sir George on the 28th. We may from *luck* (of which we have not hitherto had a common share) yet do something to retrieve our country's misfortunes; but [I] am afraid we cannot expect it from judgment or by acting by any rational well digested plan, which the present situation of things here makes absolutely necessary. Every scheme, in my humble opinion, should have been had recourse to, and every risk have been encountered to have intercepted the Brest armament; having fortunately effected that, the greatest difficulty would have been surmounted; but turn one's eyes now which way one will difficulties, and those in the extreme, stare us full in the face. How Sir George Rodney could keep his whole force to guard one path, when half of it was fully equally to the service, and to leave *another* (which appeared to me the most probable the enemy would take) without any guard at all, is matter of the utmost astonishment to me. I have really fretted myself ill, for nothing short of a miracle can now retrieve the King's affairs in this country.

On the 28th, in the evening, I received orders to proceed to this place, and anchored the next morning at sunrise. Sir George and his division came in yesterday, but Admiral Drake still remains out. I wish he was in also, that the whole might be ready to act together on the spur of the moment; for I cannot see the least service his division can do at sea, beyond that of watching the enemy at Fort Royal, which two or three frigates would do as well; and I think in the present hour no *unnecessary* risk should be run for crippling a ship of the line, as everyone will most assuredly be wanted, and their not being all together, with as few wants as possible, may be of the utmost consequence.

The force of the enemy lately arrived at Martinique is three ships of the line and three frigates, with 6,000 troops; four sail of the line parted company with the above and are gone to the Cape, and five of the line with 3,000 troops to the East Indies. All sailed from Brest together, on the 10th or 11th of last month.

Thirteen sail of Spanish ships of the line, with 9,000 troops, are said to rendezvous at Guarico, and are there to be joined by the four ships lately gone to the Cape, as well as by De Grasse (who has now thirty-three sail of the line in Fort Royal Bay ready for sea) and the Marquis de Bouillé, with the troops from Martinique, which in my humble opinion makes it highly necessary for Sir George to keep his whole force together, in as much readiness as possible, to follow De Grasse the moment he starts. Though I am writing, I know [not] when an opportunity may offer of sending; but I like to be prepared, though I should not be surprised to find a vessel is despatched to England without my knowing anything of it. Ever and faithfully yours,

SAM. HOOD.

No. I *MEMORANDUM.*

Sir Samuel Hood with his division to cruize from fifteen to twenty leagues to windward of the north end of Martinique, stretching as far north as the latitude of Dominica.

The centre division from fifteen to twenty leagues to windward of the body of the island of Martinique, stretching as far north as the latitude of the north end thereof.

Admiral Drake with his division from fifteen to twenty leagues to windward of Salines Point, stretching as far to the northward as latitude of the body of the island of Martinique.

The squadrons are to keep under such moderate sail as may be just sufficient to keep their respective stations.

One line-of-battle ship of the centre division is to be constantly stationed midway between it and the van division.

And a line-of-battle ship of the rear division is to be constantly stationed between it and the centre division.

Each squadron is to have a line-of-battle ship constantly stationed directly to windward, as far as hull down.

After having entered on their station, the squadron are to stand to the northward under the easy sail alluded to in the foregoing ; from the southern limits of their respective stations at 8 P.M., and to tack every eight hours, that they may always keep themselves at the proper distance from each other.

Commodore Affleck in the Bedford, with two sixty-four gun ships, is to cruize to windward of Guadaloupe, so as to be nearly in a right line with the other divisions of the fleet, stretching from the latitude of the north end of Dominica as far as the latitude of Deseada.

Dated on board his Majesty's ship Formidable, at Sea, the 20th of March, 1782.

G. B. RODNEY.

To Sir Samuel Hood, Bart., Rear-Admiral of the Blue, &c., &c., &c.

RODNEY TO HOOD. *No. 2.*

Formidable, at Sea, 8 P.M., 22nd of March, 1782.

Sir :—I can by no means think of keeping the fleet so much to the northward, and must therefore desire that your squadron join me, and keep in the order of sailing, as we shall thereby more easily and with greater despatch form lines of battle.

We are now off Dominica, a station I can by no means approve of for intercepting a convoy bound from Europe to Martinique. Cruizing directly to windward of that island is, in my opinion, the best method, not only of intercepting the enemy, but of protecting Barbadoes, St. Lucia, and the British trade. I must therefore beg that your division may not stand further to the northward without signal for that purpose, as I cannot by any means be induced to think the enemy will make any of the Northern Islands. A small squadron shall watch that station, but I am determined to keep with the fleet directly to windward of Martinique, and have only cruizers to the northwards.

I am, with real regard, &c.,
G. B. RODNEY.

Rear-Admiral Sir Saml. Hood, Bart
(A copy.)

HOOD TO JACKSON.

Barfleur, off Guadaloupe, 16th of April, 1782.

Private and Confidential.

My dear Sir :—I wished to have told you by the Andromache, but it was not in my power, that his Majesty's fleet had given such a beating to the *one* of France as no great fleet ever received before; and I was the less concerned at not being able to indulge my inclinations, as one of my gallant seconds (Goodall) promised me to write to you; my other second was Reynolds, and I hold myself greatly indebted to both, as well as to every captain of my division, which on the 9th sustained two attacks at a short space of time one from the other, from the whole of the enemy's van and centre, between the islands of Guadaloupe and Dominica, while the *greatest part* of our centre and every ship of the rear were becalmed under the latter; and had De Grasse known his duty, he might have cut us up by pouring a succession of fresh ships upon us as long as he pleased, but we handled them very roughly, and they being to windward hauled off, and our fleet joined in the evening. Here Sir George did exhibit much judgment in separating his fleet. The next morning the French ships were very far to windward. Sir George carried a stiff sail all day, neared them very much by sunset, and intended to have carried a plain sail all night, but by a strange blunder in Sir Charles Douglas, by making the signal for the *leading* ship to *shorten* sail, which was then under her topsails *only*, with her mizen topsails *aback*, the fleet lay to all night; at least, the centre and rear did so. Captain Byron can best tell what the van did, as he was employed the whole night in carrying messages between the *chief* and *third* in command. At daylight only a few of the leewardmost part of the French fleet could be seen from the masthead. We again worked to windward, and next morning by a lucky shift of wind we could look up three or four of the enemy's ships; this brought the whole down to succour them, and they formed on a contrary tack to our fleet. Every ship on both sides was engaged. Sir George Rodney cut through the rear of the French line so soon as my division (which was then the rear one) had passed the sternmost of the enemy's ships, which it was a long while in doing, it being almost a calm. I perceived the signal for the line of battle was down, upon which I got my boats out and towed the ship round towards the enemy, made all the sail I could (for we had soon after a little breeze), and threw out the signal for every ship of my division to do the same; and we took the Cæsar, Ardent, and Ville de Paris. Observing the Ville de Paris to edge towards the Barfleur (for every ship of the enemy was then *flying* before the wind), I concluded the Count de Grasse had a mind to be my prisoner, as an old acquaintance, and therefore met his wishes, by *looking towards him.* As soon as I got within random shot he began to fire upon me, which I totally disregarded till I had *proved* by firing a single gun from the quarter-deck that I was *well* within *point blank*, when I opened so heavy a fire against him that in ten minutes he *struck*; this was just at sunset, and my boat had scarcely got on board when Sir George Rodney made the signal and brought to, and to my very great astonishment continued to lie to the *whole night.* After the truly glorious business of the 12th, I was most exceedingly disappointed in and mortified at the commander-in-chief. In the first instance, for not making the signal for a general chase the moment he hauled *that* down for the line of battle, which was about one o'clock : had he so done (as I *did* with my division in the *only mode* I *could*) I am very confident we should have had twenty sail of the enemy's ships of the line before dark. Instead of that he pursued only under his topsails (sometimes his foresail was set, and at others his mizen topsail a-back) the greatest part of the afternoon, though the *flying* enemy had all the sail set their very shattered state would allow. In the *next*, that he did not pursue under that easy sail, so as never to have lost sight of the enemy in the night, which would clearly and most undoubtedly have enabled him to have taken almost every ship the next day. But why he should bring the fleet to because the Ville de Paris was taken, I cannot reconcile. At sunrise next morning I went on board the Formidable to pay my compliments, and to try if it was possible to recover the mistake that had unfortunately been made, and so far prevailed upon Sir George to leave the ships of his own fleet, which were most disabled, to take care of the prizes and carry them to Jamaica, and to push on in search of the enemy with the rest. Though the Barfleur and other ships of my division had a topsail yard shot in two, and in other respects much maimed, not one but chased in the afternoon with steering sails below and aloft.

Had I, my dear friend, have had the honour of commanding his Majesty's noble fleet on the 12th, I may, without the imputation of much vanity, say the flag of England should now have graced the sterns of *upwards* of twenty sail of the enemy's ships of the line.

I herewith send you copies of a few letters between Sir George Rodney and me, and had he been my father, brother, or dearest and best friend I had, I could not have *proved* myself a *better second*, or have been more open, candid, and sincere in all I have suggested to him, from my zeal and ardour for our royal and most gracious master's service, and my extreme veneration and love for his sacred person, in competition with which no consideration in this world can ever stand.

I lamented to Sir George on the 13th that the signal for a general chase was not made when *that* for the line was hauled down, and that he did not continue to pursue, so as to keep sight of the enemy all night, to which he only answered,[1] 'Come, we have done very handsomely as it is.' I could therefore say no more upon the subject. I said the same afterwards to Sir Charles Douglas, upon his paying me compliments on the management of my division. His answer was, 'Sir George chose to

[1] Compare Hotham's answer to Nelson—the standard excuse of an indolent man seeking to shirk exertion. Compare, also, Nelson's comment on Hotham with Hood's on Rodney.

pursue in a body.' 'Why, Sir Charles,' I replied, 'if that was Sir George's wish, could it have been more effectually complied with than by the signal for a general chase, with *proper attention*? Because if a ship is *too wide* upon the starboard wing, you have a signal to make her steer more to *port*. If a ship is *too wide* upon the larboard wing, you have a signal to make her steer more to *starboard*. If a ship is *too far ahead*, you can by signal make her *shorten sail*. If a ship is *too far astern*, and has not *all* her sail set, you have a signal for her to make *more* sail. And if Sir George was unwilling his ships should engage in the night, for fear of their firing into one another, the *white* flag at the foretop-gallant masthead *calls* every ship *in*, and that signal followed by the *one* for the *form* of sailing, the fleet might have gone on in sight of the enemy all night in the most compact and safe order for *completing* the business most *gloriously* the next day,' upon which he walked off without saying another word.

Indeed, my good friend, my patience is now quite exhausted, for notwithstanding Sir George Rodney appeared most perfectly satisfied, from what I took the liberty of suggesting to him on the morning of the 13th, of the great propriety of *pursuing* with all possible eagerness, and gave orders accordingly in my hearing, adding he would wait for nothing, and upon my leaving him made sail, in less than four hours he changed his mind and lay the fleet to, and here we now are in the exact same spot, off Guadaloupe. It has, indeed, been calm some part of the time, but we might have been more than twenty leagues farther to the westward.

It is a misfortune not to be sufficiently lamented that Sir Charles Douglas is so weak and irresolute.

He is no more fit for the station he fills than I am to be an archbishop. In a great fleet the duty of a *first* captain is that of being an honest and candid counsellor and adviser to the commander-in-chief; and there ought to be a most perfect, good understanding with, and confidence in, each other, which I am sorry to say is by no means the case on board the Formidable; and sure I am that if Sir George Rodney was to give orders in his cabin for any signal to be made, which would inevitably throw the fleet into the greatest confusion, or even into danger, Sir Charles has not fortitude and resolution sufficient to open his lips in remonstrance, but would most implicitly obey it.

I have been witness to his receiving orders that have appeared to my mind to be big with absurdity, and he has gone upon deck to direct their being executed, upon which I have more than once said, 'I believe, Sir George, you are unacquainted with some circumstances respecting the orders you have just given to Sir Charles Douglas, which I have related,' and he has immediately acknowledged it, sent for Sir Charles, and asked him why he had not made known what he had just heard from me, which makes the orders he has received highly improper, and they have been put a stop to. Now what I did was most certainly the *bounden* duty of the *first* captain. But all is confusion on board the Formidable, and not the least degree of attention to a regularity of system and order. Things that are of the greatest consequence to be done as expeditiously as possible are neglected, and others of a very trifling nature there is often the greatest hurry about; and orders are so frequently given one day and contradicted the next that the fleet does not get as forward in port in storing and refitting in three days as it might in one, with steadiness and a little method. In short, I am not only witness to this unpleasant and distressing conduct, but am teazed about it as often as a captain comes to me, whether if my division or not, which I am unable to remedy to any real purpose, for as often as I attempt to bring things a little to rights and succeed, it is for the *moment only*, as they never fail reverting to their former irregularity and confusion.

Sir George Rodney requires a monitor constantly at his elbow, as much as a froward child. My health has suffered very much from seeing things go as they do, for I am of that frame and texture that I cannot be indifferent where the service of my King and country is so materially affected. I must, however, endeavour to do it, or I shall be soon tossed overboard.

Sir George seems to be satisfied with having done enough, as *probably* to save Jamaica and keep his popularity alive. But, good God, not to avail himself of the manifest advantage his most *complete victory* gave him is not to be thought of with any degree of temper! We might as easily have taken the whole of the French fleet as we did the five sail (probably a ship or two might have got off, but I am confident not more than three of the line could have escaped had they been properly pursued), which would most effectually, and substantially, have retrieved all the misfortunes of poor old England, have set her on *tip-toe*, and have humbled France in the extreme. It is truly mortifying to think what a glorious turn might have been given to our royal and most gracious master's affairs, not only in this country, but at home, with only common exertion and management; and how shamefully was the opportunity neglected.

I find all this wasting of time here is to take the

Ville de Paris with him to Jamaica; such is the vanity of our commander-in-chief! He can talk of nothing else, and says he will hoist his flag on board her; would to God she had sunk the moment she had yielded to the arms of his Majesty. We should then have had a dozen better ships in lieu of her, for I am persuaded *her striking* solely occasioned the fleet to be brought to.

What think you of Sir George and his *first* captain, to suffer so great a fleet to put to sea, and in pursuit of an enemy's fleet, without a *rendezvous*, when either a victory or a defeat must have unavoidably occasioned a separation? Strange as it may appear, it is no less true; not a rendezvous was given out till the 13th, when the Royal Oak, Alcide, Centaur, with the prizes Glorieux and Hector, had parted company. Very luckily the Alert brig fell in with them, whose captain had *accidentally* heard Sir George say he would proceed to Jamaica with his whole fleet, which he made known to Captain Burnett, of the Royal Oak, so that I imagine they are gone for that island. What can we expect under such blundering conduct in matters of the highest importance to the welfare of our country, without the all-powerful hand of Providence aids us? Indeed, she has been beneficent and assisting in many instances since we left St. Lucia on the 8th, which, if I live to see you, you will I am sure acknowledge. I am most exceedingly grieved for that truly gallant and most amiable young nobleman, Lord Robert Manners—one leg gone and the other wounded, and his right arm broke; but as I think him in a good habit of body, I hope and trust he will do well. His lordship embarked in the Andromache for England, which sailed the day before yesterday. Bayne and Blair are killed, and Savage of the Hercules wounded, but not badly.

Best compliments to Mrs. Jackson and all yours, and believe me always and most faithfully

Yours,

SAM. HOOD.

Sir Samuel Hood's account of taking the Ville de Paris.

RODNEY TO HOOD.

Formidable, Tuesday Night, 9th of April, 1782.

My dear Sir :—Your public letter [1] I will answer to-morrow. I can now only say that after the very great fatigue you have undergone, which I must own has been attended with the greatest honour, I am glad to hear your health has not suffered. It will never do without we can always contrive to get the wind of the French ; they will always contrive to keep us at arm's length.

I am sorry you have lost so many petty officers. My loss, the best lieutenant I had killed, and six men besides wounded; except the two rear ships, the others fired at such a distance I returned none.

I propose, from the situation of some ships of your division, and the almost impossibility of bringing the enemy to action till we get them from under the islands, to lay to this night to give time for repairs, and to look into Guadaloupe to-morrow, and if the enemy are there to *be* at their *appointed rendezvous* before them. As I have upon all occasions the highest opinion of your judgment, favour me with it at this critical moment, and believe me with real truth Yours most sincerely,

G. B. RODNEY.

[1] To make known that Captain Bayne fell in action.

HOOD TO RODNEY.

Barfleur, at Sea, 10th of April, 1782.

My dear Sir George:—You do me great honour in holding my judgment in that estimation as to request my sentiments in the present critical moment, which I will give with that sincerity and candour I have always prided myself in doing whenever you have condescended to express a wish to know them, and if I have appeared at any time to have improperly obtruded them, I trust you will believe that zeal *alone* for the service of my King and country led me to do it.

De Grasse will certainly avoid you all he can, and when you know *not* where he is, you will, in my humble opinion, be perfectly right to push for the enemy's *appointed rendezvous*; but while you can keep him in sight, or know that he is *not* gone to *leeward*, I think you can on no account quit him, and will, I imagine, keep your fleet as much collected as possible, and avail yourself of every opportunity of getting to *windward*.

The ships the enemy's fleet had under convoy anchored at St. Pierre's, Guadaloupe, with some frigates which should be closely watched. When you are informed of the state of the Alfred you may *probably* think it expedient to send her to Jamaica, but if her masts can be secured, the ships which did not engage yesterday will be able to supply her with powder and shot.

I did not suffer a gun to be fired from the Barfleur for near twenty minutes after the Alfred began, and I think Captain Bayne was exceedingly reprehensible for presuming to fire before the signal for battle was hoisted on board the Admiral of his division, and when he was the leewardmost ship of it, and at the greatest distance from the enemy.

Your very handsome approbation of my conduct is truly flattering to me, and which I shall on all occasions be studious to merit, being with great respect, &c., &c., &c.,

SAM. HOOD.

RODNEY TO HOOD.

Formidable, Wednesday Night, 10th of April, 1782.

My dear Sir:—Many thanks for your kind advice. You may perceive my opinion coincides with yours by our endeavours to-day. I have ordered Mr. Drake to lead with a plain sail to-night, but I plainly perceive that De Grasse is unwilling to decide the affair in these seas.

I am sorry for Bayne, but own I was much hurt at seeing him fire at such a distance. Poor fellow! he is gone; and as I promised Captain Symons the first ship that became vacant, he must have the Alfred, and Lord Cranstoun the Formidable. Bouchier you may be sure will soon be post, but Vashon must be before him, as I promised in England. It gives me real pleasure to hear by Bouchier that the very great fatigue you have undergone has not injured your health. May you long continue to enjoy it is the sincere wish of,

Most affectionately yours,

G. B. RODNEY.

RODNEY TO HOOD.

Formidable, 11th of April, 1782.

My dear Sir:—My only reason for desiring you and your squadron to change stations with Mr. Drake and his was from their having suffered so much in action on the 9th, and to give you and them time to be put in repair; but, depend upon it, the moment you wish to have those directions altered it shall be done. I propose to make moderate sail this night in the order of sailing; we can easily form from that. Yours, &c.,

G. B. RODNEY.

HOOD TO RODNEY.

Barfleur, 11th of April, 1782.

My dear Sir George:—My first and greatest wish is to comply with yours. Whatever disposition you think right to make respecting my division will be most readily and cheerfully acquiesced in by me. The good of the King's service will always be a primary consideration with me. No *other* can ever stand in competition with it.

I hope we shall do most effectual business to-morrow.

I have the honour to be, &c., &c., &c.,

SAM. HOOD.

RODNEY TO HOOD.

Formidable, 12th of April, 7 o'clock P.M.

Many thanks, my dear friend, for your very kind congratulations; 'tis with the sincerest truth that I must, with great justice, acknowledge that I am indebted to your very gallant behaviour that we have been so successful. You have a right and may demand whatever officers you choose for preferment, either as captains or lieutenants.

I had wrote my letter on our first reincounter,

wherein I had done you every justice to our gracious master. To-day must add greatly to it. And I am sure there cannot be anything but you may expect from his goodness.

God bless you. Adieu!

Yours most affectionately,
G. B. RODNEY.

SIR SAMUEL HOOD'S JOURNAL.

April, Tuesday, 9th, 1782.—Fresh breezes and fair; 45 minutes past 2 P.M. the Commander-in-Chief made the signal for a line of battle abreast, which I repeated (at 2 cables' length asunder); made and shortened sail occasionally, and made several ships signals for being out of their stations; 30 minutes past 3 do. the look-out frigate ahead made the signal for a fleet, Diamond Rock, Martinique, N.E. 2 leagues; 48 minutes past do. the Commander-in-Chief made the preparative signal, which I repeated, and at 55 minutes past 3 P.M. the signal for the line abreast hauled down, and the signal for the line bearing N.E. and S.W., which I repeated; 8 minutes past 4 do. saw a strange sail in the N.E. and made the signal, which was answered by the Commander-in-Chief; 11 minutes past do. the Commander-in-Chief made the signal for all cruizers, which I repeated; 15 minutes past do. hauled down the above signal; 25 minutes past do. the Commander-in-Chief made the preparative signal, which I repeated; 56 minutes past do. I made the Yarmouth's signal to make more sail; 5 minutes past 5 do. the Commander-in-Chief made the signal for me to send out ships to chase north; 3½ minutes past do. I made the Royal Oak, Valiant and Alfred's signals to chase in that quarter; 47 minutes past 5 do. the Commander-in-Chief made the signal for the order of sailing, which I repeated; 53 minutes past do. the above signal was hauled down; at 6 do. saw two French line-of-battle ships and a frigate off the Pearl Rock, bearing north, ½ west, distance 2 leagues, and saw from the masthead 16 sail bearing N. and by W. from 4 to 6 leagues; 5 minutes past 6 ditto the Commander-in-Chief made the Canada and Prothée's signal to go ahead during the night and carry a light, and at 13 minutes past 6 do. the signal for the ships to close, which I repeated; 20 minutes past do. hauled down the above signal; 21 minutes Commander-in-Chief made the Namur's signal to shorten sail; 48 minutes past 1 A.M. the Commander-in-Chief made the signal to bring to on the starboard tack; 54 minutes past do. I repeated do.; 30 minutes past 5 A.M. the Commander-in-Chief made the signal for a line of battle ahead, at one cable's length asunder; 3 minutes past do. I repeated the above signal; 35 minutes past 5 do. the Commander-in-Chief made the signal to prepare for action; 2 minutes past do. I repeated the above signal; 50 minutes past 5 do. Commander-in-Chief made the signal for a line of battle ahead at two cables' length asunder, which I soon after repeated; at 6 A.M. saw the French fleet, with a number of vessels under convoy, bearing from N.N.E. to E., distance from 4 to 12 miles, extending from Prince Rupert's Head, Dominica, towards Guadaloupe. They appeared much scattered, occasioned by light and variable winds; at 6 do. the Commander-in-Chief made the signal for the van to fill, which I repeated, and at 38 minutes past 6 do. the signal for action was made, which I repeated; at that time none of the enemy's ships near enough to engage, and the ships in succession being taken aback, amongst which the Barfleur; 43 minutes past do. the Commander-in-Chief hauled down the signal to engage, which I also hauled down, the Commander-in-Chief made the annulling signal for do. which I repeated; 25 minutes past 7 do. the Commander-in-Chief made the signal for the van to fill; ½ minute after I repeated do. and at 30 minutes past do. the above signal was hauled down; 55 minutes past do. I made the Royal Oak's signal for being out of her station; 32 minutes past 8 do. the enemy hoisted their colours; 39 minutes past 8 do. the whole of the enemy tacked and stood on the larboard tack; 56 minutes past do. I made the Royal Oak and Alfred's signals to make more sail; at 3 minutes past 9 do. they answered do.; at 9 minutes past do. the Commander-in-Chief made the Royal Oak's signal for being out of her station; 10 minutes past do. I made the Alfred's signal for being out of her station; 48 minutes past 9 do. the enemy began to engage our van, which was returned by the Alfred, and afterwards by the van ships; 50 minutes past do. the Commander-in-Chief made the signal to engage, which I repeated, and at 6 minutes past 10 do. the Barfleur opened her fire upon the enemy; 25 minutes past do. ceased firing; 3 minutes past 11 do. backed the main-topsail for the fleet to come up; 15 minutes past 11 A.M. the Commander-in-Chief made the signal to close; 3 minutes past do. I repeated do.; 20 minutes past 11 do. I was cheered by the Royal Oak; I ordered her to be hailed, and desired to know why Captain Burnett had not made more sail, who replied he was becalmed; 29 minutes past 11 do. the Commander-in-Chief hauled down the signal for the fleet to close, which I did also, and at 40 minutes past do. the signal was made for the van to fill, which I repeated, and made the Alfred and Royal Oak's signals to make more sail; at noon employed repairing the damage sustained in action.

Wednesday, 10*th*.—Fresh breezes and clear; 5

minutes past noon, the Commander-in-Chief made the signal for the van to fill; 7 minutes past do. repeated the above signal; 25 minutes past do. hauled down the signal for the van to fill; 14 minutes past noon the enemy again opened their fire on the Barfleur; 16 minutes past do. the Commander-in-Chief made the St. Albans' signal for being out of her station; 24 minutes past do. the Barfleur opened her fire on the enemy; 40 minutes past do. the Commander-in-Chief made the signal for the rear to close the centre, which I repeated; 20 minutes 1 P.M. the Commander-in-Chief made the signal for the van to fill, which I repeated; 28 minutes 1 the Commander-in-Chief hauled down the signal for the van to fill, which I did also; saw the Royal Oak on the larboard tack, with her main topmast down; 45 minutes past 1 do. saw the Montagu bear right up, and stand to leeward of the line, at which time the Barfleur ceased firing; 55 minutes past 10 do. the Commander-in-Chief made the signal for a line of battle bearing North and South; at 2 P.M. the Commander-in-Chief hauled down the signal for battle, as did the Barfleur; at 12 minutes past 2 P.M. I made the Yarmouth's signal for being out of her station; at 3 P.M. the Commander-in-Chief hauled down the signal for the line ahead bearing N. and S., which I did also; 15 minutes past do. the Commander-in-Chief made the signal for the fleet to wear, which I repeated, and at 33 minutes past do. the signal was made for a line of battle ahead at two cables' length asunder, which I repeated; 52 minutes past do. I made the Belliqueux, Magnificent, Centaur, and Prince William's signals for being out of their stations; at 8 minutes past 4 the Commander-in-Chief made the signal for the Admiral commanding the 3rd post to tack and gain the wind of the enemy; 15 minutes past 5 do. the signal was made for the Marlborough to shorten sail; 26 minutes past 5 do. the Commander-in-Chief hauled down the signal for the line at 2 cables' length, as did the Barfleur, and at 28 minutes past do. the signal was made for the order of sailing, which I repeated; 55 minutes past 5 do. the Commander-in-Chief made the signal for a line of battle ahead at one cable's length asunder, and at the same time hauled down the signal for the order of sailing, which I repeated; at 6 do. the Commander-in-Chief hauled down the signal for the line at one cable's length asunder, and kept that for two cables' length flying, repeated do., the enemy bearing from N.E.*b*.E. to E.S.E. on the larboard tack, consisting of 33 sail of line-of-battle ships, two of which had joined since morning; at 15 minutes past 6 do. saw 40 sail of square rigged vessels, a cutter and a schooner of the enemy's; 45 minutes past 7 do. the Commander-in-Chief made the night signal for a line of battle and lay to, which I repeated; 40 minutes past 5 A.M. the Commander-in-Chief made the signal to tack, and form a line of battle ahead at 2 cables' length asunder, and made sail, which I repeated; at 6 A.M. the enemy bore from E.*b*.N. to N.E. 4 or 5 leagues, standing on different tacks; 15 minutes past do. the Alfred made the signal to speak me; at do. I made the Zebra's signal for her captain; 17 minutes past do. the Alecto spoke me and informed that the Alfred had only ten rounds of powder left; 55 minutes past 8 the Commander-in-Chief made the signal for the van to fill, which I repeated; 30 minutes past 11 do. I made the Warrior signal to make more sail; 45 minutes past 11 do. I tacked; at noon employed repairing our rigging, the enemy bearing E. ½ N., thirty-eight of our ships in company and 24 of the enemy in sight from the masthead.

Thursday, 11*th*.—Fresh breezes and fair weather; P.M. at 1, the Commander-in-Chief made the signal for the 3rd in command to make more sail, and at 35 minutes past do. made the signal for the headmost and weathermost ships to tack first; 37 minutes past 1 do. I repeated the above signal; 10 minutes past 4 do. the Commander-in-Chief enforced the above signal, which I repeated; at 5 do. the Commander-in-Chief made the signal for a line of battle ahead at 2 cables' length, which I repeated; at $\frac{1}{4}$ past 5 do. he made the Marlborough's signal to shorten sail; at do. P.M. the body of the French fleet bore E.*b*.N. 3 or 4 leagues, the extremes of Dominica E. $\frac{1}{2}$ S. off shore 5 or 6 leagues; 50 minutes past 5 P.M. the Commander-in-Chief made the Prothée's signal to chase N.E., and 52 minutes past do. made the signal for a general chase N.E.; and at 56 minutes past do. a general signal to chase to windward, which signals I repeated; at 6 do. the Commander-in-Chief made the signal for the ships in chase to tack, which I repeated, and at 45 minutes past 7 do. tacked &c. signal; at 10 A.M. could count from the masthead 22 sail of the enemy between Guadaloupe and Dominica, on the larboard tack; at noon tacked ship, saw 16 or 17 sail at anchor in Basseterre Road, Guadaloupe, 2 of which ships of the line and 1 frigate; at noon 39 sail in company.

Friday, 12*th*.—Fresh breezes and fair; 30 minutes past noon tacked and stood to the southward; 15 minutes past 4 P.M. the Commander-in-Chief made the Prince George, St. Albans, and Russell's signals to tack, and at 38 minutes past 4 do. made the Alarm, Endymion, Triton, Zebra, and Andromache's signals to come within hail; 50

minutes past 4 do. the Commander-in-Chief made the Conqueror's signal to tack, and at 54 minutes past do. the signal for all cruizers, which I repeated; 2 minutes past 5 do. the signal was made for the fleet to close, which I repeated, and at 12 minutes past 5 do. the signal was made for the order of sailing, which I repeated; 20 minutes past the signal was made for the Andromache to come within hail; 25 minutes past 5 do. the Commander-in-Chief made the signal for the 3rd in command to haul by the wind on the larboard tack, which I repeated; 25 minutes past do. I repeated the Zebra's signal for her captain; at 6 do. the Prothée made the signal of distress; 3 minutes past do. the Commander-in-Chief answered do.; at 10 minutes past 3 do. the Commander-in-Chief made the America's signal to go ahead and carry a light, and at 15 minutes past do. made the signal for the order of sailing, which I repeated; 17 minutes past do. the Alcide made the signal of distress from the condition of her masts; 41 minutes past do. tacked ship and stood to the southward, at daylight the body of the enemy N.E. ½ N. from 4 to 5 leagues, two of them considerably to leeward, about 5 or 6 miles distant; 45 minutes past 5 A.M. the Commander-in-Chief made the signal for the 3rd in command to make more sail; 50 minutes past 5 do. he made the signal for the line ahead at 2 cables' length asunder; 7 minutes after I repeated the above signal; at do. Commander-in-Chief made the signal for the 3rd in command to lead, with his division, which I repeated; 56 minutes past 5 do. Commander-in-Chief made my signal to send out ships to chase in the North; 4 minutes after I answered the above signal, and made the Monarch, Valiant, and Centaur's signals to chase to the northward; 58 minutes past do. hoisted our colours, and at 6 do. I made the Belliqueux's signal to chase N.; 15 minutes past 6 do. the Commander-in-Chief made the signal for the line of bearings, N.N.E. to S.S.W., which I repeated; 33 minutes the Commander-in-Chief hauled down the signal for the line of bearings, as did the Barfleur, and made the signal for a line of battle ahead at 2 cables' length asunder, which I repeated; 2 minutes after, at 7 do., the Commander-in-Chief made the signal for all cruizers, which I repeated; at 10 minutes past do. he made the signal for a line of battle ahead at 1 cable's length asunder, which I repeated; 15 minutes past 7 do. tacked to get into my station; 45 minutes past Commander-in-Chief made the signal to close, which I repeated, and made the Centaur's signal to make more sail; 58 minutes past 7 do. firing commenced in the van; 59 minutes past 7 do. Commander-in-Chief made the signal for action, which I repeated; 5 minutes past 8 do. he made the signal for close action, which I repeated; 8 minutes past do. the Commander-in-Chief made the signal for the leading ships to alter the course one point to starboard; 25 minutes past 9 do. the Barfleur opened her fire on the enemy, and at 45 minutes past 10 do. ceased firing, having past the enemy's van ships; at 11 do. observed the Commander-in-Chief with the signal for the line down, hauled down on board the Barfleur; 5 minutes past 11 do. I made the Centaur and Prince William's signal to chase N.W., perceived a ship of the line without a mast standing, and another with her foremast gone; at leaving off firing the Commander-in-Chief bore N.W.*b.*N.; at 15 minutes past 11 do. he made the signal for the headmost and weathermost ships to tack; I repeated the above signal; saw two of our ships to leeward of the line, one of them the Warrior, with her fore topsail yard gone; 20 minutes past 11 do. I made the signal to recall ships chasing in the N.W., and at 29 minutes past 11 do. I made the Centaur's signal to come within hail; 31 minutes past 11 she answered do.; 33 minutes past 11 A.M. the Commander-in-Chief made the signal for the headmost and weathermost ships to tack; 35 minutes past 11 do. I repeated the above signal; at noon the sternmost ships of my division still in action; employed refitting the rigging and making all the sail I could.

Saturday, April 13th, 1782.—Moderate and clear weather; employed making sail and getting down the main topsail yard, it being shot in two, got another up; 20 minutes past noon observed two of our ships engaged to leeward, and at 30 minutes past do. I observed the Commander-in-Chief with the signal for the van to close the centre, which I repeated; 54 minutes past noon I made the Alfred's signal for a lieutenant; at 1 P.M. the Commander-in-Chief made the signal for close action, which I repeated; 30 minutes past 1 do. I perceived one of the enemy's ships without her masts had struck, at the same time saw the Commander-in-Chief with his main topsail to the mast; at 32 minutes past 1 do. he filled and hauled down the signal for close action; at 37 minutes past 1 do. I made the Centaur and Prince William's signals to make more sail; 40 minutes past do. the Montagu's signal to make more sail; 50 minutes past 1 do. Magnificent's signal to tack; at 52 minutes past 1 P.M. I made the Prince William's signal to alter her course to starboard; 53 minutes past 1 do. I made the Centaur and Montagu's signal to alter their course to starboard, which was immediately answered; 58 minutes past 1 do. made the Magnificent's signal to make more sail; at 2 do. set the main topsail and studding sails; 8 minutes past 2 do. I made the Warrior's signal to make more sail; at 16 minutes past do.

the Centaur and Valiant's signal to make more sail; 21 minutes past 2 do. observed the Commander-in-Chief with the Royal Oak's signal to take possession of the enemy's ship which had struck; 35 minutes past 2 do. I made the Monarch's signal to come within hail; 13 minutes past 3 do. observed the Commander-in-Chief with the Bedford's signal for being out of her station; 15 minutes past 3 do. a line-of-battle ship struck to the Centaur; 21 minutes past 3 do. I made the Belliqueux, Valiant, Montagu, and Prince William's signals to alter their course to starboard; 22 minutes past 3 do. observed the Commander-in-Chief with the Marlborough's signal to make more sail; 28 minutes past 3 do. I made the Yarmouth's signal to make more sail, and at 35 minutes past do. made the Montagu's signal to chase west; 45 minutes past 3 do. the Commander-in-Chief made the signal for the ships to windward to bear down into his wake, which I repeated immediately; 48 minutes past 3 do. observed the Commander-in-Chief with the Repulse and Monarch's signals to bear down into his wake; at 4 P.M. the Commander-in-Chief made the signal to wear, repeated, and hauled down the signal to bear down into his wake; 10 minutes past 4 do. the Commander-in-Chief hauled down the signal to wear, as did the Barfleur, and at 12 minutes past do. he made the Namur's signal to make more sail; 20 minutes past 4 do. observed a line-of-battle ship of the enemy strike to the Canada; 25 minutes past 4 do. I made the Valiant's signal to make more sail, and at 30 minutes past do. the Yarmouth and Belliqueux's signals to make more sail; P.M. 33 minutes past 4 the Commander-in-Chief made the Conqueror's signal to make more sail; 40 minutes past 4 do. saw the Formidable with her main and fore topsails to the mast, a boat from her appeared to be going on board the ship which had struck to the Canada; 45 minutes past 4 do. she filled again; 48 minutes past 4 do. the Commander-in-Chief made the Marlborough and Conqueror's signal to bear down into his wake, and at 50 minutes past do. the Fame and Agamemnon's signals were made to bear down into his wake; 10 minutes past 5 do. the Commander-in-Chief made the Fame's signal to make more sail; 25 minutes past 5 do. observed the Commander-in-Chief make the Princesa and Hercules' signals to bear down into his wake; 28 minutes past 5 do. Commander-in-Chief made the Namur's signal to make more sail; 45 minutes past 5 do. a line-of-battle ship of the enemy struck to the Belliqueux; 53 minutes past do. Ville de Paris began to fire at the Barfleur; 55 minutes past do. I made the Valiant's signal to alter her course to starboard; 5 minutes past 6 do. the Barfleur opened her fire on the Ville de Paris, and at 29 minutes past 6 do. the Ville de Paris, of 110 guns, struck to the Barfleur; 45 minutes past 6 do. the Commander-in-Chief made the signal to bring to on the larboard tack, hoisted out a boat and sent an officer with a party of men to take possession of the prize; ½ past 6 A.M. filled; ¾ past 7 do. brought to; at 8 do. thirty-six sail in sight, and 10 from the masthead to the westward; at 11 ditto filled and made sail in company with the Commander-in-Chief and part of the fleet.

LOG OF H.M.S. CANADA.

Tuesday, April 9th, 1782.—Fresh breezes and cloudy; at 3 P.M. the Admiral made a distant signal 5 times, and the signal to form the line of battle ahead; ½ pt. 3 the Admiral hoisted a blue flag with a white cross from corner to corner at the foretop masthead; at 40 minutes pt. 3 he hoisted a blue flag pierced with white at the mizen peak, and fired 2 guns; a frigate ahead made the signal for a fleet; at 4 the Admiral hoisted a white flag at the foretop masthead; ½ pt. 4 he hauled down the signal for the line and made the signal for a general chase; at 6 the Admiral made our and the Prothée's signals to keep ahead during the night; the Endymion, Andromache, and Alarm went also ahead; at 7 the W. wt. most part of Martinique distant 4 or 5 leagues; saw 2 ships running along shore to the northward; the Admiral having made the signal for the 2nd in command to send ships out to chase, Rear-Admiral Sir Samuel Hood sent the Royal Oak, Valiant, and Alfred to chase to the north-west; ½ pt. 10 three sail passed us on the larboard tack, made and shortened sail occasionally; A.M. at 20 minutes pt. 3 the fleet bore S.S.E. 3 or 4 miles; at break of day saw a convoy with some men-of-war off Prince Rupert's Bay, Dominica; at 5 beat to quarters; Prince Rupert's Head E. and N. about 5 leagues; ½ pt. 5 the Admiral made the signal for the line of battle ahead, but being near the land the whole fleet were becalmed; at 40 minutes pt. 5 he made the signal to fill, the van first; at 18 minutes past 6 he made our signal to engage, one of the enemy's ships being at that time becalmed not far from us; at 24 minutes pt. 6 he made the signal to annul, the ship having got a breeze and joined the French fleet; at 6 minutes pt. 7 he made the signal to fill, the van first; at 7 minutes pt. 7 beat the retreat; got into our station in the line; 35 minutes pt. 8 Rear-Admiral Sir Samuel Hood made the Alfred's signal to make more sail; at 45 minutes pt. 8 the Admiral made the Royal Oak's and Magnificent's signals to get into their stations; ¼ pt. 9 the Admiral made the Alfred's signal to make more sail; at 25 minutes past 9 beat to quarters; ½ past 9 the van of our fleet began to fire at the centre of the enemy's; 37 minutes past 9 the Admiral made the signal that the rear squadron were at too great a distance from the centre; at 43 minutes pt. 9 we fired 2 shot at one of the sternmost of the enemy's ships to try if they would reach, but they falling short we ceased firing; at 15 minutes pt. 10, one of the enemy's ships having wore and edged a little down, we began to fire; at this time the Admiral, with the Namur and all the ships astern of him, were becalmed from 6 miles to 4 leagues astern; at 35 minutes past 10 the firing ceased on both sides; counted the enemies fleet, which consisted of 29 ships of the line and 4 frigates, and 2 sail close in with Dominica, which we take to be line-of-battle ships; at 50 minutes past 10 the Admiral made the signal to close; at 10 minutes past 11 the Admiral made the St. Albans' signal to get into her station; ¼ past 11 the Namur, Formidable, and Duke, having got the wind, came up and began firing at the sternmost ships of the enemy's rear, which they returned; at 18 minutes past 11 Rear-Admiral Sir Samuel Hood made the signal for the van to fill; our rear lying still becalmed astern; at 42 minutes past 11 we fired several shot to try the distance; ¾ pt. 11 the Admiral hoisted a yellow flag at the foretop masthead; at 50 minutes pt. 11 the van of our fleet exchanged a good many shot with the enemy's; at 55 minutes pt. 11 the Admiral made the signal to fill, the van first; at noon the Admiral made the St. Albans' signal to get into her station; fresh breezes and cloudy.

Wednesday, 10th.—Fresh breezes and cloudy; at 5 minutes P.M. the firing ceased between the sternmost ships of the enemy's rear and part of the centre of our fleet; at 12 minutes P.M. the Admiral made the signal that the rear were at too great a distance from the centre; observed the Belliqueux with her mizen topmast gone; at 55 minutes P.M. the Admiral made the signal to fill, the van first; at 20 minutes pt. 1 observed the Royal Oak (with her maintopmast gone) had bore out of the line; at 22 minutes pt. 1 the Admiral made the signal to form the line of bearing No. and So. 2 cables' length asunder; at ½ pt. 1 the firing ceased betwn. the van of our fleet and that of the enemy's; at 33 minutes past 1 the Admiral hauled down the signal for battle and made the Andromache's and Alarm's signals to come within hail; made and shortened sail occasionally; ¾ pt. 2 the Admiral made the preparative signal; at 55 minutes past 2 he made the signal to wear; at 10 minutes pt. 3 wore the whole fleet together; ¾ pt. 3 the Admiral made the signal for the line of battle ahead, made and shortened sail occasionally; at 20 minutes past 3 he made the Alert's signal to come within hail; ¾ pt. 3 he made the signal for the Commander in the 3rd post to tack and gain the wind of the enemy; ½ pt. 4 the Admiral made the Endymion's signal to come within hail and the Marlborough's signal to shorten sail; at 5 he made the signal to form the order of sailing; ½ pt. 5 he made the signal to form the line of battle ahead; made and shortened sail occasionally; unbent the mainsail and bent a new one, the old being damaged by shot; at 6 brought to and repaired the main topmast, and set it; at 8 fresh breezes and cloudy; A.M. at 4 fresh breezes and clear; at daylight the French fleet just in sight from the deck to windward, and the Alarm halfway between the two fleets; ½ pt. 5 the Admiral made the signal to fill, the van first; at 6 the Admiral made the signal to tack. Repaired the several shot holes in the staysails, made and shortened sail occasionally; at 9 the Admiral made the Hercules' and Prothée's signals to make more sail; Rear-Admiral Drake made the Arrogant's signal to get into her station; the Admiral made the signal to form the line of battle ahead a cable's length asunder; tacked; at 10 the Admiral made the signal to fill, the van first; made and shortened sail occasionally; at noon the Admiral made the Prothée's, Resolution's and Hercules' signals to make more sail.

Thursday, 11*th*.—Fresh breezes and clear; P.M. the Admiral made the signal for the commander in the 3rd post to make more sail, and the Prothée's signal to shorten sail, and soon after the Prothée's and Resolution's signals to get into their stations; $\frac{1}{2}$ pt. 3 Rear-Adm. Drake made the Arrogant's signal to shorten sail; at 4 tacked pr. signal; at 5 the Admiral made the signal for the line of battle ahead; $\frac{1}{2}$ pt. 5 he made the Fame's, Hercules' and Prothée's signals to make more sail; at 7 the North end of Dominica E.N.E. 4 or 5 leagues; at 8 tacked, made and shortened sail occasionally; $\frac{1}{2}$ pt. 9 brought to; $\frac{1}{4}$ pt. 10 the Admiral hoisted two lights at the ensign staff and one at the mizentopmt.-head, and fired 2 guns; at 10 fresh gales; lowered the topsail on the cap; A.M. fresh breezes; at 2 the Admiral made the signal to tack; filled; at 4 fresh gales and cloudy; at 5 the Admiral made the signal for a general chase to windward, and for the ships before his beam to tack; at 6 tacked; unbent the main topsail, it being split, and bent another; at 8 tacked, unbent the jib, it being split, and bent another; counted 33 sail of the enemy to windward; at 9 observed the Warrior with her main topmast gone; saw 2 line-of-battle ships, 3 frigates, and several merchant ships in Fort Royal Bay, Guardaloupe; at 11 tacked, and stood to the southward; at noon fresh gales and cloudy.

Friday, 12*th*.—A.M. at ½ pt. 4 a schooner from the Admiral passing by hail'd us, and said he had a letter from the Admiral for Captain Cornwallis; we brought too, but she went astern, and we saw her no more; saw the French fleet to leeward of the Saints; at 5 the Admiral made the signal for the line of battle, and for the 3rd in command to lead; observed a frigate with a French line-of-battle ship (much disabled forward) in tow steering for Guardaloupe; at 10 minutes past 5 the Admiral made the signal for the 2nd in command to send ships out to chase to the N.W.; Sir Samuel Hood made the Valiant's, Centaur's, Monarch's and Belliqueux's signals to chase in that quarter; at 20 minutes to 6 the Admiral made the signal for the line of bearing N.N.E. and S.S.W.; at 35 minutes past 6 the Admiral altered the signal for the line of bearing to that for the line of battle ahead; moderate and cloudy; ¼ past 7 the Admiral made the signal for all cruizers; at 20 minutes pt. 7 he made the signal for the line of battle ahead a cable's length asunder; the enemy formed in line of battle ahead upon the larboard tack, and standing to the southward, and we formed the line of battle ahead upon the starboard tack, and stood to the northward; at 8 the Admiral made the Russell's signal to get into her station; at 5 minutes pt. 8 he made the signal to close; at 50 minutes past 7 the van of our fleet began to engage; the Admiral made the signal to engage close; ¼ past 8 the Admiral began to engage, as did all the ships as they came abreast of the enemy; there was a great interval in the enemy's line; our fleet cut through to windward of about 12 ships of them; at 20 minutes past 8 the enemies ships as they passed began firing at us; at 25 minutes past 8 we began to engage; at 20 minutes past 9 one of the enemy's ship's main and mizen masts went over the stern just as she got abreast of our quarter, and soon after her foremast and bowsprit fell; also at 25 minutes past 9, having passed the enemy's fleet, some of whom went to leeward of us, the Admiral made the signal to tack; $\frac{1}{2}$ past 10 the Admiral hauled down the signal to engage; at 38 minutes past 10 he hoisted do., and made the signal for the commander in the 3rd post to make more sail; observed the Duke's maintopmast go over the side; at 50 minutes past 10 observed the Prince George with her foremast gone; we ceased firing, as did most of the ships on both sides, except Sir Samuel Hood with part of his squadron, who were to windward, and exchanged a good many shot with the enemy as he bore down; at 11 observed that the Admiral had hauled down the signal for the line; at 5 minutes past 11 the Admiral made the signal to tack; wore; $\frac{3}{4}$ pt. 11 fired several shot at the enemy to try the distance, but finding they did not reach, ceased firing; at 50 minutes pt. 11 the Admiral made the Conqueror's signal to tack; made and shortened sail occasionally.

SIR SAMUEL HOOD TO LORD ROBERT MANNERS, IN LONDON.

Barfleur, off Altavela, St. Domingo, 22nd of April, 1782.

I most sincerely hope and pray this may find your Lordship as well as your unhappy misfortune will possibly allow, and that you may be restored to perfect health. From the Andromache, where I paid you my respects, I went to the Formidable, and as the various methods I had tried were ineffectual to induce Sir George Rodney to quit the Ville de Paris and pursue the flying enemy, I added the following *P.S.* in answer to a note he sent me:—'As I understand the Royal Oak, Alcide, and Centaur, with the prizes Glorieux and Hector, are gone towards Jamaica, will they not be in great danger from *our* being so far astern?' This brought me a letter from Sir George, of which I send a copy.

Now where was Sir George's judgment to subject me, with only *ten* sail of the line, to fall in with twenty at *least* of the French, and at the same time to keep twenty-two sail with him to take care of the Ville de Paris, without the shadow of a prospect of meeting a single ship of the enemy's? The French fleet, which your Lordship had so large a share of glory in putting to flight on the 12th, to the number twenty-six, including frigates, passed the Mona Channel *only* the day *before* I was in it. If divine Providence was not to assist us, as it has most kindly done in many instances since we left St. Lucia, what would become of our poor distressed country? It is painful to think of, and I have not patience, my Lord, to dwell longer upon so truly mortifying and much to be lamented subject, but will just observe to your Lordship that on the morning of the 15th, finding Sir George could not bring himself to lose sight of the Ville de Paris, I pressed him much to add half a dozen ships of the line and a couple of frigates to my division, and allow me to pursue the *flying* enemy, and pledged myself to give him a good account of them. His answer was, 'We will make all sail as fast as we can,' to which I replied, 'You will be too late, depend upon it, if you wait for the Ville de Paris;' and when I last saw the Commander-in-Chief, on the 17th at sunset, he was laying too with his whole fleet. *Seal of arms.*

Endorsed [by the Duke of Rutland].—'Received June 19. My dearest Bob died of his wounds, April 23, 1782.'

HOOD TO JACKSON.

Barfleur, off Altavela, St. Domingo, 22nd of April, 1782.

My dear Jackson:—After trying every method to no sort of purpose to induce Sir George Rodney to *quit* the Ville de Paris and pursue the flying enemy, in answer to a note he sent me on the 17th in the morning, I added the following *P.S.*:—'As I understand the Royal Oak, Alcide, and Centaur, with the prizes Glorieux and Hector, are gone towards Jamaica, will they not be in great danger from *our* being so far *astern*?'

This brought me a letter from Sir George, of which No. 1 is a copy, and No. 2 is the copy of my public letter to him of this date.

Now where, my good friend, was Sir George Rodney's judgment to subject me, with *only ten* sail of the line, to fall in with twenty at *least* of the French, and to keep at the same time with him *twenty-two* to take care of the Ville de Paris, without the least prospect of his meeting a single ship of the enemy's? The French fleet, which that noble one of his Majesty's had put to flight on the 12th, to the number of twenty-six, including frigates, passed the Mona Passage on the 18th, *only* the day *before* I was in it. If divine Providence was not to assist us, as it has so kindly done in many instances, what would become of our poor distracted country? It is dreadful to think of, and I have not patience to dwell longer upon a subject so truly mortifying and to be lamented; and will only add that on the 15th, in the morning, I expressed my wish to Sir George that he would give me half a dozen ships of the line and a couple of frigates to my division, and allow me to pursue the flying enemy, and pledged myself to give a good account of them. His answer was, 'We will all make sail as fast as we can;' to which I replied, 'You will be too late, depend upon it, if you wait for the Ville de Paris;' and when I last saw the Commander-in-Chief, on the 17th at sunset, he was laying to with his whole fleet.

I am, my dear Sir, with all good wishes to Mrs. Jackson,

Your most faithful and obedient,

SAM. HOOD.

Off Port Louis, St. Domingo, 24th of April.

When I left Sir George Rodney on the 17th he sent me a message that a ship would go in five or six days with his duplicate despatches, but not till I rejoined, and desired me to have my letters ready; and upon my going on board the Formidable on the 22nd I found the Eurydice had sailed for England on the 18th. What dependence is there upon the word of such a man? And how is it possible to keep one's temper with him? He frets me to death. I am to wait here till he brings the *Ville de Paris up.*

RODNEY TO HOOD, ENCLOSURE I.

Formidable, 17th of April, 1782.

My dear Sir:—I should be glad [if] you with your squadron would go as far ahead as hull down, and keep so till we get as far as Altavela; we shall steer W. ½ S. till we get to that place, which is about midway of St. Domingo on the south side, and I am sure we shall overtake the Royal Oak, &c.; but if you think otherwise, which I submit to your better judgment, please to make sail till you get abreast of Altavela, and there wait till we join. The sooner we proceed the better.

Believe me to be, with regard and real truth,

My dear Sir, yours, &c.,

G. B. RODNEY.

HOOD TO RODNEY, ENCLOSURE 2.

Barfleur, at Sea, 22nd of April, 1782.

Sir:—In obedience to your commands, expressed in the letter you did me the honour to write me on the 17th, to make sail with my squadron, and submitting it to my judgment whether to stop upon my getting hull down from your fleet, and go on at that distance till we got off Altavela, which is midway of the island of St. Domingo on the south side, or to push on till I reached the length of Altavela, and there wait your coming, I immediately made all the sail I could, and judging the only chance I had of intercepting any stragglers of the *flying* enemy was to be off the Mona Passage as soon as possible, I carried steering sails below and aloft, night and day, and on the 19th at daylight made the west end of the island of Porto Rico, soon after which the Alecto fire-ship, which was some distance ahead, made the signal for a fleet in the North-West. I immediately threw out the signal for a general chase, and at sunrise five sail were seen from the masthead of the Barfleur. About five hours after we got so near them as plainly to discover they were French ships, and two if not three of them of the line, and as they then saw what we were they steered for the very narrow and unfrequented channel between Porto Rico and the little island of Zacheo, in which four were overtaken.

Between two and three in the afternoon the Monarch began an action with the nearest ship of the enemy, and the Belliqueux was close after her when they were taken aback, and by baffling winds fell astern, while the French ship, though within point blank shot, carried a little breeze; but the Valiant attacking her she soon struck, and Captain Goodall immediately pushed after another of the line, not far from her, which made a gallant defence for an hour and then struck, her commander finding he could not succeed in his endeavours of running her on shore. About this time the Magnificent took L'Aimable, a very fine large coppered frigate whose captain resisted full half an hour, and almost at the same moment the Champion took the Ceres, a very elegant little coppered ship, late his Majesty's sloop Ceres, close to the shore. The fifth separated in the forenoon and steered to the westward, which the Warrior was directed to pursue, and she was afterwards followed by the Prince William; so soon as the prizes were taken possession of and the prisoners partly shifted, I made the signal and bore away out of the narrow channel.

It is a very mortifying circumstance to relate to you, Sir, that the French fleet which you put to flight on the 12th (twenty-six in number, including frigates) went through the Mona Channel on the 18th, only the day before I was in it.

Herewith is an account of the killed and wounded on the part of his Majesty, as well as that of the enemy, with the names and force of the ships taken and the number of men each had on board. Every one of them was loaded with shells and other ordnance stores, amongst which are forges complete for red-hot balls at a siege.

The Caton and Jason are very fine ships, almost new; were built at Toulon, which last twice as long as those built at Brest.

The Valiant as well as the last ship she took were much hurt in their masts, yards, sails and rigging, but both are now to rights and fit for immediate service.

I have the honour to be, with great respect, Sir, your most obedient and most humble servant,

SAML. HOOD.

HOOD TO JACKSON.

Barfleur, off the Isle Navassa,[1] 30th of April, 1782.

Private and Confidential.

My dear Sir:—On the 25th in the forenoon I joined the commander-in-chief off the isle La Vache. We proceeded together as far as Cape Tiberon, when he parted for Jamaica, with the following ships, Formidable, Prince George, Duke, Fame, Russel, Ajax, and Hercules, of the line, and Flora frigate, and captured ships, leaving me to cruize with twenty-six sail, but I have only twenty-five with me, the Warrior not having joined; but I know she did not come up with the ship I sent her to chase.

I suppose Sir George Rodney got to Port Royal yesterday, if not the day before; so soon as I hear from him I am to detach the Ceres home—at least such was his determination when he left me.

How Sir George has disposed of all his frigates I cannot guess, for he had seldom one with him but the *repeaters*. He took the Eurydice, Admiral Drake's repeater, to carry his *duplicate* despatches; and though twenty-six sail of the line require three repeaters, one for each division, the Champion is the only one now in the squadron, and no frigate of any sort besides. I do not feel pleasant on that score, thinking it not only proper but highly necessary the combined fleet at the Cape should be narrowly watched, which cannot be done but by stout, fast sailing frigates; and I am not free from apprehensions that, if the enemy should judge an attack upon Jamaica not prudent or practicable,

[1] A little island between the western end of Haiti and Jamaica. It is about thirty-one miles west of Cape Tiberon. La Vache, the buccaneer island of Ash, is off Abacou Point.

which I think very likely, the French may return with part of their ships and troops to windward, knowing, as they must, that we have no force there to resist whatever they may attempt. We cannot, therefore, be too diligent in looking out and guarding against any feasible plan. There is another most material object we ought to have an eye to, *that* of the enemy's going to America, by putting his Majesty's squadron in a condition to follow as expeditiously as possible; at present it is very far from being so, as no one ship is perfect in her masts and yards, or without wants of various kinds; and I am free to confess I can see no real service my keeping the sea is of (beyond what a couple of frigates could perform) with a *crippled* squadron, and so inferior to the enemy, should the resolution of attacking Jamaica with all their force not be given up; for we have certain accounts that there were on the 17th at the Cape thirteen Spanish and five French ships of the line, with 8,000 Spanish troops, very impatiently waiting the arrival of De Grasse's squadron from Martinique, since which twenty-five sail of French have joined, making in the whole forty-three of the line, and I should imagine the latter carried about 4,000 troops.

Now, had Sir George Rodney's judgment, after the enemy had been so totally put to flight, bore any proportion to the high courage, zeal, and exertion so very manifestly shown by every captain, officer and man under his command in battle, *all* difficulty would now have been at an end. We might have done just as we pleased; and instead of being at this hour upon the defensive, a force might have been preparing to return to the Windward Islands for the purpose of attacking the enemy's possessions there, with the fairest prospects of success.

Surely there never was an instance before of a great fleet being so *completely beaten* and *routed* and *not pursued.* So soon as the Ville de Paris had struck, Sir George's faculties seem to have been benumbed, farther than respected that ship *alone*; and I am every day more and more convinced, by the declarations of officers then on board the Formidable, that the Ville de Paris being taken was the sole occasion of the fleet being *brought to* and laying *to all night.* Had it been my lot, my dear friend, to have commanded his Majesty's fleet on the 12th, and have passed by so clear and very favourable an opportunity of raising the glory of my country, as I am grieved to say *was done*, I should have thought my head would have been justly required for such a glaring and shameful neglect. My feelings are so strong that I must express myself so *to you* (trusting I write to *you alone*), to give vent to the perturbation and anguish of my mind; and sooner than undergo for a continuance what I have so very painfully done for several weeks past, I would be content to be placed on a Welsh mountain to gather *buttons* as they drop from a goat's tail.

Did you write me by the Fury? If you did, I have not received your letter. She joined us on the 26th at night.

Adieu! With best regards to Mrs. Jackson,

I am most truly and faithfully yours,

S. H.

Don't put any letters to me under Sir George's cover.

HOOD TO JACKSON.

Not yet through the Gulf of Florida, 21st of August, 1782.

Secret and Confidential.

Surely, my dear friend, we seem somehow or other to be strangely infatuated. The Jamaica convoy joined us on the 14th, in the afternoon, upon which we bore away to the westward the whole night, and though not a single ship of it was to be seen at daylight from the masthead, we continued to run before the wind till the evening, and then lay to; since which we have loitered very much, carrying moderate sail in the daytime, and only under our topsails in the night. This looks as if we were totally inattentive how the time slipt away, and how exceeding precious it is to us; and instead of leaving a frigate to take care of, and follow with four or five paltry prizes, they are, it seems, to be *towed* all the way to New York in company with the fleet. How very tedious will this make our passage! When not a moment should be lost, whether we find the enemy in force upon the American coast, or are to seek them in a more southern latitude, despatch, in my humble opinion, in either case is absolutely necessary and of great consequence.

When the Spaniards were found so *strong* and *ready* at the Havannah as to make it expedient that the convoy should pass the Gulf before us, his Majesty's fleet should have cruized between Cape Antonio and the dry Tortugas, not only for intercepting anything to the Havannah but to have cut off all intercourse from the island to the Bay of Campeachy, as we had undoubted intelligence that ships with treasure were daily expected. Instead of that we kept to the eastward near the Matanzas, and suffered ships from Cadiz to get in, which sailed in company with two that had fallen into our hands: and though a clear knowledge whether the Spanish General Don Bernardo Galvez was left at the Cape is of the utmost consequence to us, we are still in total ignorance of it. But the fleet should not have shown itself off the Havannah, or even in sight of Cuba, but at some distance in the rear of the convoy, and the Jupiter and a frigate been sent to reconnoitre, which could not have failed procuring that information, so very proper and important to us; for so soon as our fleet was seen, it is natural to suppose an embargo was laid on, and express boats sent off from the outports to stop the treasure ships, &c., from the Main, and not a ship of ours was stationed to the westward of the Havannah.

I suppose the convoy is now above forty leagues ahead, when we surely should not be further astern than just to keep sight of the tail of it from the masthead; and as the Commander-in-Chief could not be brought to approve of sending a squadron equal to Vaudreuil's to precede the convoy, I concluded he would have left a sufficient number of ships with Admiral Graves to have insured protection to the charge he had with him into the latitude of Bermuda, and then have pushed on himself with the rest of his fleet to New York, causing the Chesapeake to be looked at by his scouting frigates; for admitting he thought it probable he should find the enemy superior to him in America, he might have directed the flag-officer he had detached to look out for him, at any bearing and distance he pleased from Cape Henry; and I think each squadron would have got there about the same time, since he *tows* the prizes with him; and had Admiral Pigot arrived first and judged it right not to wait, but to proceed on to New York, he had only to have left a frigate upon the rendezvous to give the information. But doubtless he may have very solid and substantial reasons for what he does from the tenor of his instructions, which I cannot be supposed to know. One circumstance strikes me very forcibly, that seems not to be properly attended to. The Magnificent has been on shore, lost her false keel and gripe, keeps her hand-pumps going night and day without ceasing, and must be hove down. In this situation she ought by no means to be carried into action, yet she is still with us, though she might at this hour have been at Halifax (where I understand she is intended to go), and would probably have joined before we left New York; as it is, she is likely to become liable to an equinoctial gale before she reaches her careening port.

I really cannot help feeling very much for Admiral Pigot, and probably have gone too far in hints I have thrown out to him, though I must confess he has given me no reason to suppose he has not taken all I have said in good part, and a single moment's reflection must have convinced him I could have no other view than his interest; but he seems at present to have no other idea than carrying his fleet altogether to New York, without considering that a part of it might probably answer full as effectually for the King's service as the whole, and regardless (if one may be allowed to judge from appearances) how long he is going thither. His situation is much to be pitied, having no one about him capable of affording wholesome advice, which, without the smallest imputation to him, as he has been so long on land and never hoisted his flag or commanded a squadron before, I should think could not be unwelcome. I unbosom myself to you, my dear friend, and write without reserve; fully confiding I address myself to you *alone*. I prepare this letter in case a sudden opportunity should offer. I have been confined to my cabin several weeks and cannot shake off my complaints; but not a word of this, for if my wife should know it she will be miserable. I am very uneasy. I had no letter from you or any part of my family, and cannot help having strong suspicions on that score.

With all affection to you and yours, Adieu!

24th of August.

On the 21st in the afternoon we got a fair wind, which carried us through the Gulf in the course of the night, but at daylight we brought to, continued to lie to till noon, and afterwards only went under our topsails, because a little prize polacre was missing, which astonished all I have seen, and leads them to conclude the fleet has been delayed from a consideration to a few hundred pounds. When I took the liberty of suggesting to Admiral Pigot, a long while ago, whether it was not advisable to leave a ship to bring the prizes on, his answer was they would never get to New York if they are not *towed*. Why, far better would it be they never should than that the fleet should be detained a single day on their account. Very fortunately yesterday afternoon we fell in with a small schooner from Charleston, charged with despatches from General Leslie to General Campbell at Jamaica, upon which I received a note from the Admiral informing me the French squadron had been seen ten days ago in latitude 38° 10′, steering to the northward, supposed for Rhode Island; why not for New York? For though I do not think it very *probable*, yet it is *possible*, particularly as we are told the island of New York is invested by an American army. The idea is distressing when we might have been ahead of the enemy with a far superior squadron, with a fair prospect for intercepting them. It is pretty evident Vaudreuil has cruized for the Jamaica convoy (as the day fixed for its *positively* sailing was the 10th of July, which was published long before in all the newspapers, and was as well known at Cape François as by our own merchants and planters), and probably to the first part of this month, for having been seen entering the windward passage on the evening of the 3rd of last month, he cannot have made the best of his way. We might have had six- or seven-and-twenty of the line at sea so soon as the combined fleet left the Cape (and which we should have had between the 5th and 10th but for the information received of Admiral Pigot's coming, which so disturbed the Commander-in-Chief he knew not what he was about, for I was told day after day from the 5th I must sail next morning), and upon finding the Spanish squadron at the Havannah, six or eight ships might have been left off Cape Antonio to wait for the convoy, which would have strengthened Admiral Graves sufficiently to have insured his safety into the latitude of Bermuda; and even late as Admiral Pigot sailed, sixteen of the line at least might have been at New York a fortnight ago, with full protection for the convoy left behind.

The intelligence by the express boat brought Admiral Pigot to a determination to wait no longer for the prizes, and in order to take good care of them he left the Endymion, Southampton, and Sybille for their protection, when the *former* and the little German sloop would have been a sufficient safeguard to them; but this proves how very intent the Commander-in-Chief is on securing his property in the prizes; but if officers cannot be found that will make the glory of their King and country to take place of every other consideration, there is no salvation for us. The labour and toil of a few will not effect it. The principle must be adopted in common, and strictly attended to by men in authority and command, or all is over with poor old England as a great nation. I confess that I like the aspect of things less in the West Indies than before the 12th of April, for if Vaudreuil is come this way just to show himself, and *wear* away the hurricane months, I fear he will have the start, and be gone back again, long before we shall be ready to follow him, unless we are very alert indeed. I pray God my apprehensions may be groundless, and that on our getting to New York I may have good reason to view things in a more favourable light

In answer to the note Admiral Pigot sent me, I took the liberty of hinting the necessity of his sending away a frigate immediately to reconnoitre the Chesapeake, that he might not be unnecessarily delayed an hour off Cape Henry. I also suggested another frigate to be instantly despatched to New York to announce his near approach, and to desire Admiral Digby would cause a sufficient number of pilots to be collected on board the guardship at the Hook, with two small sloops or schooners to buoy the channel so soon as the fleet appeared, as the loss of a tide may occasion a delay of many days; and that Admiral Digby might likewise be desired to order the contractor to have as many bullocks ready to kill, and as much spruce beer brewed as possible, that the poor seamen may not be a day without all the refreshments that can be procured them, or otherwise they will probably be a week and not have any.

If the commander-in-chief of a great fleet does not upon every occasion look forward, the crews of it will be often deprived of what they stand in need of, are entitled to, and might have.

It has been my misfortune to bury thirty-nine men since the day the Barfleur anchored at Port Royal, exclusive of the badly wounded, which were found room for in the hospital. I brought 140 out in fevers and fluxes, which the sea air very much assisted in bringing about again, but I have now but few short of that number in the scurvy, very bad, and must be put on shore as soon as possible, or most of them will die. If a man strikes one leg against the other, or meets with the least accident so as to break the skin,[1] annleer (*sic*) soon forms, and a mortification very rapidly follows without the greatest care; the juices of the poor fellows are in so bad a state. I stand in need of many refreshments also, but very much flatter myself the smell of the earth and constant exercise mornings and evenings, when we get in upon Long Island, if it should be safe to ramble there, will so far set me up as to enable me to hold out this campaign. To see things go so very *slack* and *untoward* cannot but affect a man in this country in the highest health, and it is impossible for *one* afflicted as I am with strong bodily complaints to bear up against them. Since I wrote the sheet on the 21st, I find my poor wife must have been under great trouble for the loss of her good old father. I had not a line from her or from my son or daughter by the Lively brig, which has vexed me sorely, and it was in a newspaper of the 18th of May I saw an account of Mr. Linzee's death.

[1] Anuli? In scurvy a dark ring, similar in colour to a bruise, forms in case of the kind of accident Sir Samuel speaks of, and leads to sloughing, which is what he probably means by mortification. The dark spots in scurvy are, properly speaking, called 'petechiæ.'

25th of August.

The Fortunée departed for the Chesapeake and the Jupiter for New York last night, which they ought to have done many days ago, and there is no accounting why it was not so, but from the indolence and dilatoriness which prevail on board the Formidable. There is doubtless something very wonderfully mysterious in the Chief's conduct, which I own I have not penetration to fathom, and the more I think of it the more I am bewildered. Strange as it may tell, it is no less true, though we have been six weeks at sea, and *loitering* the whole time, not one single manœuvre has been practised—no, not even spreading in a line abreast (since we came through the Gulf) at a mile or two distant in the day and closing a little at night, by way of exercising the fleet, which surely was highly necessary, if only for the better chance of procuring intelligence of the enemy and how matters stand at New York, &c.

29th of August, Lat. of Cape Henry.

In a few hours after we parted with the prizes, I saw reason to suspect the appearance only of despatch in getting forward was meant; circumstances since have justified my suspicions, for they have been in sight every day, and at daylight yesterday morning, the Sybille and a little polacre were ahead of the fleet, the rest not far behind. This proves very strongly the different frames of men's minds; some are full of anxiety, impatience, and apprehension, while others, under similar circumstances, are perfectly cool, tranquil, and indifferent. Mine is of the former cast, and I confess that from the moment it was known a French squadron was ahead, I should have considered the fleet in chase till it got to Sandy Hook; not from any expectation of overtaking the enemy, but that not a moment might be lost in putting his Majesty's ships in a condition for sea again. Having one-third of the Barfleur's ship's company down in the scurvy, a hundred very bad indeed, and six or eight dropping into the list every day, I thought it very much my duty to send a report to the Admiral, and to desire his permission to make the best of my way to New York, that my poor fellows may be put on shore as soon as possible, as a single day may be saving the lives of many. But is it not singular that an account of the state and condition of the fleet has not been called for since the day the commander-in-chief left Port Royal, upwards of six weeks ago? Many ships, I know, are unfit to be at sea, and as things appear to be circumstanced, would it not be far better they should be in port? It is really ridiculous to see the *whole* kept out doing nothing, and nothing in all likelihood to be done that *half* would not be equal to.

I parted at eight last night, and shall harbour as expeditiously as I can. But what think you of the commander-in-chief at Jamaica? The captain of the frigate which last came from thence says he has detained the Warrior, one of Admiral Pigot's ships, to send her and the London on a cruize together; but I own I cannot credit it—surely the London is of no more use upon that *station* than a stout frigate would be; though, between ourselves, our friend Jos[1] is not a very unlikely man to take an inconsiderate step, from the little I have seen of him. You must know I met him at sea as he came out of Port Royal, and saluted him with thirteen guns, to which salute he only returned eleven. Should you not, I

[1] Sir Joshua Rowley, who commanded at Jamaica between the departure of Sir Peter Parker in the summer and the return of Admiral Pigot to the station in the autumn of 1782.

replied, have given me gun for gun, agreeably to the fourth article of the regulations and instructions relating to his Majesty's service at sea respecting salutes? He answered he ordered eleven only to be fired, but not out of any disrespect to me. I then said I did not mention it as a personal matter, but that he was certainly wrong, which he must acknowledge. The gentleman took exception, it seems, at my wearing a flag of the same colour as his own (which I had an order to do from the commander-in-chief, and which I also now have from Admiral Pigot, as has Admiral Drake to wear a white one, for the better distinguishing the divisions), as you will see by his answer (which I herewith send) to a letter I thought it my duty to write him, that I might show to my corps, and to the world, I was not insensible to any failure of that respect the flag I had the honour to wear was entitled to. Here I thought it prudent to let the matter drop; but I own it has not made a very favourable impression on my mind of our friend's judgment. I never saw him at sea before.

30th of August.

This morning I spoke with the Jupiter in her way *to* New York, her captain having thrown out a signal for the purpose after making the *private ones*, taking my flag for Admiral Digby, not thinking it possible for the Barfleur to be ahead and to windward of the Jupiter. When Captain Pasley came on board he told me, among other circumstances, that he had been informed by the master of the polacre he took on the 5th, in the night, near the Havannah, that he received intelligence the evening before, by a boat which came off to him, that an express was arrived from Cape Corrientes with an account that the English convoy was in sight from thence, and that all the men-of-war at the Havannah were preparing to sail—indeed, their appearance plainly showed it; so that you see, my good friend, what a chance we have lost of taking and destroying the whole by our so injudiciously showing our force to Solano's view, instead of keeping to the westward, to have fallen into the rear of the convoy, and sending frigates to reconnoitre the Havannah.

Captain Pasley yesterday spoke with the Centurion, four days from New York, and was told by her commander the French squadron of thirteen of the line is arrived at Boston; if the information is correct as to the number, only ten Spanish ships must have sailed from the Cape and thirteen French, in place of thirteen of the former and ten of the latter, as we were informed at Jamaica, for the whole consisted but of twenty-three of the line.

In a conversation when I delivered a certain paper I sent you by the convoy, and of which you have now a duplicate, I suggested an alternative, that if a squadron was not detached to precede the convoy in quest of Vaudreuil, as many ships might be left to join Admiral Graves as would give him a superiority to the Spanish squadron at the Havannah, or to the French one, in case of his meeting it before he reached the latitude of Bermuda, and for the rest of the fleet not to lose a moment's time in getting to New York, as it was highly probable the good people there had their fears very much alive, and possibly under very alarming difficulties. Do you think, my good friend, a certain noble Viscount[1] has acted upon true *patriotic* principles, as a real friend to his poor distracted country, in placing an officer at the head of so great a fleet so very unequal to the very important command for want of practice? Had he shown the least degree of foresight and judgment, and been possessed of that spirit of

[1] Keppel.

enterprise which, I am grieved to say, the present moment so much requires, he might have had a very noble chance for rendering a good account both of the French and Spanish squadrons. His *force* was equal to, and (not only in my opinion, but in the opinion of many others) fully justified the attempt, but he could not be brought to relish a separation of his fleet; and had we not loitered from the 17th to the 25th between Port Royal and the west end of the island, the Monarch would have been with us, and the Magnificent not disastered. But, admitting the necessity of waiting, it should have been *off Port Royal only*, and a frigate sent in with a letter to Lord Rodney from Admiral Pigot, expressly to say he only waited for the Nonsuch and Anson in place of the Warrior and Repulse to proceed. This would have been coming to a certainty at once; instead of that we ran down off Savannah La Mar, which would lead Lord Rodney to imagine we were gone on, and most probably occasioned his Lordship to take the two ships through the windward passage with him; but his doing so, or depriving the convoy of that strength he might have given it, and which it ought to have had, can on no score be justified.

I believe, my dear friend, I am too open and honest-hearted to live in the present times, and my mind often tells me I express my thoughts too freely; but I cannot help it, particularly when I am writing to *one* I flatter myself has a real regard for and will not *commit* me.

I am the more astonished at the very dilatory moving of the fleet, as Admiral Pigot on his arrival at Jamaica most perfectly coincided with my ideas, that not a single moment was to be lost in getting to New York, and what can have occasioned such an alteration in his sentiments I am puzzled to conceive, or even to guess at.

3rd of September.

I am just anchored at Staten Island, and as I will not attempt to say a word of matters here, will only add my best wishes to you and yours.

I am your very sincere friend,

HOOD.

5th of September.

The July packet arrived, and brings an account of Lord R[ockingham]'s death and of Lord S[helburne] being gone to the Treasury, that Messrs. Fox and Burke have resigned, and that Lord K[eppel] and the Cavendishes have done the same or about to do so. Lord T[emple] and Mr. T[homas] T[ownshend], Secretaries of State; Mr. Wm. Pitt, Chancellor of the Exchequer; and Sir G[eorge] Y[onge], Secretary at War; Lord H[owe] named for the Admiralty. That his Lordship was at sea, and had gone between Scilly and the Land's End to get *without* the combined fleet; so that I think we may soon hear of a battle. God grant the arms of his Majesty may be victorious!

I suggested to Mr. Digby whether it would not be advisable for a squadron superior to Vaudreuil *immediately* to make the round of Boston Bay in its way to Halifax to water and refit, which would [put] a check upon the enemy, and give countenance to our friends. The Admiral approved very much, and wrote a letter to A[dmiral] Pigot upon the subject, which was sent by a frigate before the fleet reached the bar; but I fear the measure will not be adopted.

7th of September.

The fleet *within* the bar, and the *prizes* in *three* days before it.

Adieu!

After detaining the Warrior a week, the commander-in-chief very wisely paid attention to the humble remonstrances of her captain and others, and suffered her to proceed agreeably to Admiral Pigot's orders. She and the Invincible joined off the port, and are now at the Staten Island.

It being beyond a doubt that Admiral Don José Solano and his squadron are at the Havannah, I very much wish to be certain whether Don Bernardo Galvez, with any considerable number of Spanish troops, were left at the Cape, or returned with the Spanish Admiral before we pass the Gulf of Florida.

Now the question is, What can be Vaudreuil's plan with the squadron he put to sea in company with the Spanish Admiral?

If he is gone to America he will have done his business before we can get there, and be secure against any attack, unless he can be met with in deep water.

But is it unlikely that Vaudreuil may have an eye upon the Jamaica convoy, and the *captured* line-of-battle ships? The object must be confessed to be very tempting. And may not Don José Solano have retreated to the Havannah on the same motive in order to take a double chance? For if he had not some *immediate* design in view, would he be laying at this season of the year with all his ships in that perfect readiness for sea?

Having turned all circumstances in my mind very seriously, I will candidly express my thoughts.

The King's fleet now consists of twenty-four of the line, the Jupiter and four frigates. I would have a flag officer, with ten or eleven sail, the Jupiter and two frigates, push away towards Bermuda, and cruize forty or fifty leagues to the South-West of the island for fourteen or sixteen days, then repair to New

York, and the rest of the ships, after the convoy is through the Gulf, to go to that port, reconnoitring the Chesapeake in its way. This latter squadron would thereby probably be watered by the time the other arrived, which would prevent delay and much confusion, as the *powers* of New York are by no means equal to the completing so large a fleet at one and the same time. Suppose, then, there is no object for his Majesty's fleet upon the American coast; it shall in that case put to sea again as soon as is practicable, and make the best of its way off Cape François, before which port one half[1] should cruize with a 50 gun ship and a frigate between the Cape and the Mona Channel, and the other half between the Grand Caicos and Inagua.

This would give a very fair chance for preventing a junction between Solano and Vaudreuil, admitting an attack upon Jamaica is still intended; and upon receiving intelligence to be relied on that the design of an attack is abandoned, the fleet should push away to windward. But a frigate should be immediately despatched to Barbadoes, whose captain should be strictly ordered to New York as expeditiously as possible; and another frigate, or the Leander, should be directed from that *quarter* to cruize for the fleet, between Cape François and the Grand Caicos, that the Commander-in-Chief may not be ignorant of the state of the enemy, and of the Windward Islands. But should Vaudreuil be found harboured upon the American coast, a sufficient force must be left to watch him, and the rest of the fleet should proceed off Cape François, to guard that port against Solano's entrance, or Vaudreuil's, should he slip by the squadron cruizing against him.

[1] The Invincible and Warrior are daily expected to join, and the Nonsuch and Anson will come to us at New York.

N.B.—In conversation when I delivered this I suggested an alternative, that if a squadron was not to *precede* the convoy in quest of Vaudreuil, as many ships might be left to join Admiral Graves as would give him a superiority to the Spanish squadron at the Havannah, or to the French *one* in case of his meeting it before he reached the latitude of Bermuda, and for the rest of the fleet to proceed to New York as quick as possible, as it was highly probable the good people there had their apprehensions very much *alive*, and probably were under very serious and alarming difficulties.

HOOD TO PIGOT.

Barfleur, at Sea, 22nd of November, 1782 (off Sandy Hook).

Sir:—I am extremely happy to tell you that his Majesty's squadron, under my command, is safe over the Bar.

Upon talking with some officers who have served many years upon the Jamaica station, I find the French always go out into the sea through the Caicos Passage, though seldom or ever return that way back, but go to windward of the Silver Keys, and make Cape Samana, on the east end of Hispaniola. And Captain Nelson, of the Albemarle, who has been cruizing about the Caicos Channel for ten or twelve weeks at a time, does not remember to have seen a ship of any burthen coming to Hispaniola by that passage. The reason against the channel inward is doubtless strong and good, as the making it from the northward must depend upon the longitude being exact, and the French, I believe, are not adepts in that knowledge, and if they fall but a few leagues to leeward they will not be able to fetch to windward of Cape Nicola Mole, from which they may be some time in getting to Cape François.

Upon this account, as you are pleased to submit the King's squadron to my discretion and judgment, I think the chance will be far better for intercepting Vaudreuil's squadron off the Old Cape, a little to the westward of Cape Samana, than off Caicos Island, and I shall then be in a fair way of meeting with any reinforcements coming from Europe or Martinique, which may be expected, and also of joining you, should you judge it necessary to come to leeward. For these reasons I flatter myself you will approve my changing my rendezvous to the east end of Hispaniola, and trust you will do me the justice to believe that I am actuated only in doing so from thinking it most advisable for the good of the King's service.

Small merchant vessels, as well as privateers, often pass the Caicos Passage from America, but it appears to me hazardous for a squadron to attempt to hit it, bound to a port rather to windward, for fear of falling to leeward, and they would be less likely to be correct in their longitude by having merchant ships under convoy.

I shall despatch a frigate to cruize off the Caicos Island, to inform any captain of a ship that may come there to look out for me where I am, and in case of falling in with the enemy's squadron to push forward to me as fast as possible through the Caicos Passage.

I have the honour to be, Sir,

Your most obedient and most humble servant,

HOOD.

[*A Copy.*]

HOOD TO JACKSON.

Barfleur, off Cape Tiberoon, 29th of January, 1783.

My dear Jackson:—By the Alcide and Prince William, which joined me on the 11th instant from Barbadoes, I received two affectionate letters from you, one of the 5th of July and the other of the 8th of August; but surely there must be letters somewhere from you of a prior and subsequent date. By the same conveyance I had the pleasure of above one hundred others, which were consoling to me beyond expression, as I had received but one short letter from any part of my family of a later date than the end of April, which was a serious concern to me; however, I had then the satisfaction of knowing all were well on the 5th of November. What an escape have I had in the affair of Westminster! And how judicious and wise has my son acted in withdrawing my name as a candidate! There are many folks, my dear friend, who *like sport* to gratify particular passions, but few regard what befalls the man who makes it; and though I am not insensible to the unmerited hostile attack of Mr. Fox, I feel myself indebted to him as the instrument of my being saved from ruin, for I do solemnly declare, poor as I undoubtedly am, I would sooner have given 500*l.* than have stood a contest, even had I been sure of succeeding for one-twentieth part of the money. A seat in the House of Commons I have no ambition after, and will never *offer* myself for it *anywhere.* If there should be public spirit enough left in any corporation in England to make choice of me as its representative —well, if not, I shall be full as well satisfied. I shall ever most carefully and studiously steer clear, as far as I am able, of all suspicion of being a *party man*, for if once I show myself of that complexion, whether for or against a Minister, unbecoming a military servant to my Royal master, I must from that moment expect to lose every degree of consideration in the line of my profession, which ever has been, and ever will be, the first and greatest object of my wishes. I revere my King, I have much affection for my country, and the pride and glory of my remaining days will be to assist both to the utmost extent of my feeble abilities; and I am vain enough to think myself in some degree qualified by a knowledge of my duty, but much more so from inclination to fight the battles of my country upon my own element, but am free to acknowledge myself totally unfit to fight the battles of a Minister in a House of Parliament; and even if I had abilities equal to the undertaking, I think it an employment derogatory to the true character of a sea officer, whose highest ambition is to stand fair in the good opinion of his Sovereign and fellow subjects.

These are my real sentiments, and I hope and trust I shall never want fortitude sufficient to adhere to them.

I am grieved beyond expression to find, notwithstanding the change that has taken place amongst the King's Ministers, that such cruel distraction still continues, as it must most infallibly sooner or later work our ruin. We have accounts of peace from various quarters. It is an event I shall have cause to rejoice at on *many accounts* with respect to myself, but whether I shall have reason to do so on the score of my own country I very much doubt, being clearly of opinion, *all things duly considered*, formidable as the combination most undoubtedly is against us, we shall, I fear, never again be in so good a condition for retrieving the nation's splendour as at this present moment. Nothing is wanting, I am very confident, to effect it but perfect unanimity at home, and a regard into whose hands the King's fleets and armies are trusted. Without that *all* is over with us as a great and powerful kingdom, and it matters not whether we have peace, or [whether] war continues; it will come to the same point, with this difference only, that by peace the evil will be placed at somewhat a greater distance, but, according to my conception, equally sure and certain; and if it shall please God to prolong my life to another war, I shall look to the event of it with fear and trembling, unless by the all-powerful interference of Providence we become a *united* and *rational* people. After a few years' peace we shall have scarce a lieutenant that will know his duty. At present our situation is bad enough in that respect; it will then be abundantly worse, as we have so many *ignorant boys* in that station (I speak now with regard to the King's fleet in these seas), which from being any time on shore will, of course, become more ignorant, and probably not so well disposed to improve themselves, and the few capable officers we now have will then be past active service.

My opinion of the sad *finish* of the 12th of April is well and fully known to every officer in the fleet, as I declared it to the Commander-in-Chief on board the Formidable the next day, in the presence of *several*, three of which went home in the Andromache; and I am confident it is by no means singular, but pretty unanimously concurred in. That gallant, good officer, Captain Cornwallis, can give perhaps a better and more just account of the transactions of that day than any other person, as his situation enabled him to do so. Notwithstanding this, I am free to acknowledge the force and propriety of your advice, though I am no *time server*, but keep in mind an old *adage*, that *honesty is the best policy*, however out of fashion it may now be.

At midnight on the 11th of this month I was joined by the Actæon, one of Rear-Admiral Rowley's ships, which I had taken upon me to station to the northward of the Caicos Passage, to look out for the much expected *Marquis*, whose commander informed me he had on the 8th, in the afternoon, discovered a large fleet steering for the Passage, which was either French or Spanish, and that he counted fifteen very large ships, and afterwards saw a frigate with French or Spanish colours hoisted bear down, and speak to two neutral ships he had boarded that morning. I immediately examined how the winds had been between the 8th and 11th, and finding no fleet could fetch Cape François, I concluded it would steer for Cape Nicola Mole or the Bight of Leogane, and bore away, though I was pretty confident in my own mind (and told Captain Parry so) the fleet seen was the transports from Charleston going to Jamaica; but he was so positive of its being either French or Spanish, and that fifteen were of the line, I was under the necessity of attending to his information; but neither seeing nor hearing anything of an enemy's ship, and after ordering two frigates to reconnoitre Cumberland Harbour, the only place a squadron could take shelter in, I hastened back to my station to windward of the Cape, and very fortunately nothing had arrived but an American frigate from Europe, which after tarrying a few hours proceeded for the Havannah.

On the 19th at night I received certain intelligence that the Marquis de Vaudreuil was off the harbour of St. John's, Porto Rico, on the 16th with ten sail of the line. I immediately did my utmost to get to windward, but wind and current were both so strong against me, I could gain but little ground. On the 23rd I was informed the enemy was still off St. John's on the 21st. On the 24th, at three in the morning, a large French ship with masts and 250 soldiers on board came under the stern of my repeater, taking us for the French squadron. She sailed from Portsmouth, in New Hampshire, on the 29th of last month, with the Auguste, Pluton, and Amazon frigate, and parted company with the two line-of-battle ships in a South-East gale and snow-storm three days after they came out, and were informed by a pilot off St. John's, on the 22nd, that Vaudreuil had gone to leeward the night before, on being joined by the Auguste and Pluton, and upon the return of the Amazon's boat from the shore she bore away also, after ordering the transport into St. John's, but on her working up to the harbour's mouth a sudden squall carried away her maintop mast, which caused her to bear up for the Cape and to fall into our hands. Upon receiving this intelligence I made all possible sail to the westward, taking it for granted Vaudreuil had gone through the Mona Channel, with a design either of harbouring at Port Louis on the south side, or coming round the west end of the island to Nicola Mole, or into the Bight of Leogane, unless he should go to the Havannah to join Don [José] Solano, and come in great force together to the Cape, which I think not at all unlikely; and though I was well satisfied the French squadron could not have passed me unseen, I thought it right to look into the Cape and the Mole as I came down.

I have now but a small chance indeed for a meeting with Vaudreuil, but in order to enable the King's squadron under my command to keep the sea ten or twelve days longer, I availed myself of a few hours' calm to distribute a little water and provisions to those ships which were most in want, some having only two days' bread and but a few tons of water. We have had no supply of the latter since the 14th of November, and when we reach Jamaica not a ship will have more than two or three days of bread, flower, pease, rum, or water. But I thank God we are tolerably healthy, though the scurvy has taken root in two or three ships. Twelve weeks will be a long time to be at sea in this country, more particularly as the squadron is so very short of water casks. I left the America and two frigates to keep an eye upon Cape François, and have sent the Prince William to reconnoitre Port Louis. When she returns I must make the best of my way to Port Royal, leaving the Alcide and Prince William to take the America's station, as that ship as well as the frigates will be obliged, from their wants, to be in port by the 10th of next month, which will probably be about the time I *must* be there also.

If upon Sir Richard Hughes's arrival at Barbadoes from Lord Howe, the Commander-in-Chief had not seen it necessary to keep that force to windward, and had come with or detached it hither, St. John's in Porto Rico, as well as Cape François, might have been guarded, which must have secured Vaudreuil to us; but doubtless Admiral Pigot had good and sufficient reason, from his information from home, against doing either. The force to windward is twenty-three if not twenty-four of the line, and the Leander; if, therefore, nothing was to be apprehended but from the French squadron from America, ten sail might have been spared, and a superiority left to Vaudreuil. But it was next to a certainty that his destination was for the Cape, to make a junction with the Spaniards, who were to have been there the end of last month; but an account of the evacuation of Charleston and New York had reached the Governor of the Havannah's ears, which made him to protest in the most solemn manner against Don [José] Solano's leaving the port; however, Admiral Pigot might have strong reason to expect a very formidable force at the Windward Islands from France or Spain, though I am free to confess my opinion that, let the enemy's force which may come from Europe be more or less formidable, it will not touch at Martinique but come directly to Hispaniola. But when an officer in command does that which human prudence as well as sound judgment directs, he ought to submit with all becoming fortitude; there is no resisting the decrees of Providence. I always write to you fully and freely, trusting I may safely do so. On the return of the two frigates I sent to examine Cumberland Harbour, where they saw nothing, I got a certain account that my conjecture to Captain Parry was right, for the fleet he saw and made report of to me was the transports from Charleston, under convoy of three frigates, neither of which ever saw the Actæon. This will show what sad consequences may arise from a loose report of a fleet that is not looked at near enough clearly to ascertain whether it consists of men-of-war, or merchant ships. I am the more concerned on this occasion, as Captain Parry is universally esteemed a solid and judicious officer, notwithstanding the mistake he lately made.

Port Royal, 6th of February.

I arrived here yesterday and found many letters up to December 5th, but not a line from you. A packet is about to sail, and I have now much to do. I will therefore only add kindest regards to Mrs. Jackson, and am, my dear Sir,

Very faithful yours,

HOOD.

HOOD TO STEPHENS.

Pall Mall, 13th of November, 1783.

Sir:—I must beg to trouble you to lay before the Lords Commissioners of the Admiralty a detail of a very serious nature to me. When I had the honour to command the King's fleet in Carlisle Bay, Barbadoes, in December, 1781, the French fleet under the Count de Grasse was then at sea, with a body of troops on board, beating up to Barbadoes to attack the island; and his Excellency the Governor, judging it expedient to lay on a close embargo, and making an application to me to assist that very necessary service, in order to prevent intelligence from going to the enemy, I ordered Captain Lucas, of his Majesty's fireship the Salamander, to Speights's, a bay on the west part of the island, and to use his best endeavours to prevent any vessel putting to sea from that place. The Dumfries, a ship from the coast of Guinea, Mr. Alexander Currie, master, was then laying there, who, in opposition to the remonstrances of the officers of the island, and of Captain Lucas, commander of the Salamander, after furling the ship's sails with rope yarns in the evening cut her cables when the day was closed, and pushed to sea. Captain Lucas followed in the Salamander, and brought her back to Carlisle Bay. For what passed between the two ships I must beg to refer their Lordships to the several affidavits of the persons which I now transmit.

The King's Attorney-General at Barbadoes was made acquainted with all the circumstances of the affair, who said he thought the behaviour of the master and crew of the Dumfries of too atrocious a nature to be properly punished abroad, and that a special commission would issue in England for trying the offenders, and advised that Mr. Alexander Currie, the master, and his mates, should be kept confined.

So soon as the ship Dumfries was brought into Carlisle Bay, I wrote to a Mr. Shirley, to whom I understand the ship was consigned, and told him I was much concerned for what had happened, and very desirous that the owners should suffer as little as possible through the delinquency of the master; that I wished him to do whatever he thought best on the part of the owners, in which he should have all the assistance I could give. He accordingly sent people on board to take charge of the ship, and she proceeded for, and arrived safe at, Jamaica, at which island a Habeas Corpus was procured for the removal of Mr. Currie and the mate to the shore, where the former was admitted to bail, himself in a bond of 500*l.* and two sureties in 250*l.* each, and Captain Lucas was bound in 300*l.* to prosecute, who attended to bring the matter to issue, but through evasion on the part of Mr. Currie no trial ever came on, though Captain Lucas was removed from the ship he commanded to attend [to] that business, and when the mate was carried on shore he was rescued, and no bail given for his appearance.

On my arrival in town last night, I was informed an action was brought against me by a Mr. Robertson, late a victualling office clerk, and then owner of the ship Dumfries, for the sum of 5,000*l.*, for taking out the men from the said ship, and refusing to return them when applied for.

Under the above circumstances I flatter myself their Lordships will think it but reasonable and just that the Admiralty solicitor be directed to defend me. Had I been guilty, Sir, of any act of oppression, I should have been ashamed to make application to their Lordships; but if an officer in the due execution of his duty, and for the good of the King's service, is not protected by the Crown against attacks of this sort, his situation is piteous in the extreme. In the meantime, I have been under the necessity of ordering an appearance in my behalf, or judgment would be given against me for default in three days.

I have the honour to be, Sir,

Your most obedient and most humble Servant,

HOOD.

INDEX

PRINTED BY
SPOTTISWOODE AND CO., NEW-STREET SQUARE
LONDON

THE NAVY RECORDS SOCIETY

PATRONS

H.R.H. THE DUKE OF SAXE-COBURG AND GOTHA, K.G., K.T. &c.
H.R.H. THE DUKE OF YORK, K.G. &c.

PRESIDENT

EARL SPENCER, K.G.

THE NAVY RECORDS SOCIETY, which has been established for the purpose of printing rare or unpublished works of naval interest, aims at rendering accessible the sources of our naval history and at elucidating questions of naval archæology, construction, administration, organisation and social life.

In 1894 the Society issued two volumes of *State Papers relating to the Defeat of the Spanish Armada*, edited by Professor Laughton.

The volumes for this year will be :—

Letters of the first Lord Hood from the West Indies in 1781–2, edited by Mr. David Hannay;

An Index to James's Naval History, presented to the Society by the Hon. T. A. Brassey; and

A Memoir of Captain Stephen Martin, the brother-in-law and companion in arms of Sir John Leake, written by his son, Stephen Martin Leake, edited by Mr. Clements Markham.

For next year the volumes will probably be :—

The Journal of Rear-Admiral Bartholomew James, during the Wars of American Independence and the French Revolution, edited by Commander J. Y. F. Sulivan; and

Mr. Holland's *Two Discourses on the Navy*, written about 1639 and 1660, edited by Mr. J. R. Tanner.

Other volumes in preparation are :—

Navy Accounts and Inventories under Henry VII., to be edited by Mr. M. Oppenheim ; Roll II. of *The Declaration of the Navy*, by Anthony Anthony, to be edited by Professor Elgar ; and the Journal of Sir George Rooke (1700–2), to be edited by Mr. Oscar Browning.

Any person wishing to become a Member of the Society is requested to apply to the Secretary (Professor Laughton, King's College, London, W.C.), who will submit his name to the Council. The Annual Subscription is One Guinea, the payment of which entitles the Member to receive one copy of all works issued by the Society for that year.

June 1895.

1045528R0

Printed in Great Britain by
Amazon.co.uk, Ltd.,
Marston Gate.